300
CHRISTIAN AND
INSPIRATIONAL PATTERNS
for Scroll Saw Woodworking

BY THOMAS L. ZIEG

Fox Chapel Publishing
Box 7948
Lancaster, Pennsylvania 17604

Author Dedication

*This book is dedicated to those
who played a role in my Christian upbringing.*

Acknowledgment

As with most major undertakings, the culmination of the project does not lie with the efforts of one individual. I would like to express my gratitude to those who provided information or in any way helped with the production of this book. First, I wish to thank the Lord, whose existence made this book a possibility and reality. Thanks to my wife Judy and daughters Andrea and Rebecca for their feedback, patience, and support for the project. I also want to express appreciation to Alfred and Thelma Zieg, Gary and Nancy Heinicke, Jim and Dawn Zieg, Victor and Joretta Borcher, and Robert (Bob) Ewell for their efforts and assistance.

Special appreciation is given to Allena Lewis for taking time from her busy schedule to review many of the drawings and provide much needed constructive criticism and insight.

The list would not be complete without extending my gratitude to the staff of Fox Chapel Publishing Company, Inc. for allowing me the opportunity to write this book.

Publisher: Alan Giagnocavo
Cover Design: Robert Altland, Altland Design
Photography: Bob Polett, VMI Communications

Manufactured in the United States of America

ISBN # 1-56523-063-9

To order your copy of this book,
please send check or money order for cover price plus $2.00 to:
Fox Chapel Book Orders
Box 7948
Lancaster, PA 17604-7948

Try your favorite book supplier first!

CONTENTS

INTRODUCTION

Using a scroll saw can be a very satisfying and stimulating form of relaxation. With a scrollsaw, a woodworker can turn scrap wood into beautiful gifts and useful household items.

The objective of this book is not to explain how the scrollsaw works or how to use it. This book is not aimed specifically at the scroll sawing newcomer. Many books explaining the saw and providing information on basic operation written by well-known and respected practitioners already exist in the marketplace. See the Bibliography for a listing of some of those books.

This book is intended more for the person who has some knowledge of and experience with the scroll saw.

Some of the projects can be completed with just the scroll saw. Most of the projects will require the use of a hand or electric drill. However, a selection of easy projects are included to help the beginner succeed while increasing his/her confidence and ability. Many medium to complex patterns intended for the more experienced scroll sawer are also included.

This book is simply about ideas. An endeavor has been made to present a series of designs along with their symbolism to enable the reader to understand how the designs were derived. It is hoped that the beginner and experienced alike will find something of interest herein.

The woodworker should not feel confined to using the patterns exactly as illustrated. The patterns may be changed to meet specific needs by reducing or enlarging.

Cutting out many of the patterns in this book produces very delicate or fragile parts. A very fine blade is a necessity. The woodworker must have good control and cut carefully and slowly. .

To cut the patterns in this book, I use a 16" 2-speed scroll saw. The slower speed setting provides the control needed to make the intricate cuts required by the patterns. Using the slow speed extends the time necessary to complete the project, but it also ensures the project turns out nicely.

I used an assortment of different blades in my scroll saw. I made the intricate lettering cuts with a very fine-tooth blade (27 teeth per inch). Although the blade is designed for cutting thicknesses up to 3/32", the slow speed allows much thicker wood to be cut.

Usually, you should make the interior cuts of the patterns first. Work from the center of the pattern outward to avoid putting pressure on the areas already cut. Each smaller element of the pattern should be cut from the inside out, just like the overall larger pattern. This method of cutting becomes particularly important for lettering. See the example below.

Cut in the direction of 1-4

If the outside of the letter was cut first, the saw pressure and vibration could break the appendage off at the narrow connecting bridge. Cutting the outside last will give the appendage the support needed.

I hope this book brings you much pleasure and enjoyment as you learn from each design and make your own woodworking heirlooms.

SCROLL SAW MANUFACTURERS

Delta International Machinery
246 Alpha Drive
Pittsburgh, PA 15238

Seyco Sales
Excalibur Saws
1414 Cranford Drive
Garland, TX 75041

Hegner Scroll Saws
Advanced Machinery Imports
Box 312
New Castle, DE 19720

Penn State Machinery
2850 Comly Road
Philadelphia, PA 19154

RB Industries
1801 Vine
Harrisonville, MO 64701

SYMBOLISM

The use of symbols to convey abstract ideas is as old as the world. With no printed word, cultures relied upon symbols to communicate. A variety of languages and dialects within a language also dictated the need for universal symbols.

Many of the Christian symbols developed hundreds of years ago to tell the story of Christ still have meaning today. They are found in traditions and teachings, on church windows and furnishings.

This book describes some of the more common symbols. Other exist. The reference section of this book contains sources of additional information.

Symbolism is a universal language that expresses abstract ideas through suggestion. The word symbol is derived from the two Greek words, syn, meaning together, and ballein, meaning to throw. The symbolon, or symbol, becomes a mark that joins together and abstract idea and a likeness to an object or experience. Through association, the mark, no matter how trivial, becomes a story much deeper than meets the outward appearance.

The language of symbols served a real need in the early Christian church. There was no printed word. Also, there was a variety of languages and dialects, Christians depended on symbolic language to recapture the story of Christ and His promises. They also used symbols to provide a secret language during periods of persecution.

Today, symbolism is still an important part of the elements of Christian faith, tradition, and teachings. The use of symbols on church windows and furnishings present an interesting and valuable pictorial supplement to preaching and religious education.

Christians have utilized many different symbols to proclaim their faith. To give a complete description of those symbols would require more pages than is the intent of this book. Included here are only those symbols which are used in the design of the patterns in this book.

Although many symbols are religious symbols, it is important to remember that a "religious" symbol is not necessarily a "Christian" symbol. Symbolism is as old as the world and many symbols belong to pagan religions. Prior to the development of any "Christian" design, verification should be made of the symbols used and their association with the Christian faith. In using Christian forms and symbols, three worthy virtues of their use should be noted: reverence, simplicity, and sincerity. This book may be used as a reference for some of the more common symbols. Additional information may be found by referring to the reference section of this book. Other symbols may be discovered by reading the writings of the prophets.

CROSSES

The simplest cross is an upright stake having one or more cross pieces. Used in the time of Abraham as a method of capital punishment, it became an image of pain, guilt and disgrace.

After Christ was crucified on the cross, Christians adopted it to signify a servant and follower of Christ. That meaning continues today. The cross also signifies redemption through the death and resurrection of Jesus.

In wider terms, the cross represents the union of opposite because of the horizontal cross pieces joined to vertical ones.

The cross belongs to no one religious denomination. More than 400 various shapes of the cross exist today. This book includes only a small portion of that number.

OTHER SYMBOLS

ANCHOR: It is a secret sign of the early church, with the cross as part of the anchor. If the church is a ship, it must have an anchor.

ANGEL: The most misunderstood and abused subject in Christian art. Messengers of God, angels should be properly represented as beardless, sexless winged beings in human form with bare feet.

Angels are spirits created by God before the world to serve him.

Although they exist in a different dimension from the physical, visible world we know, they may assume bodies.

Angels are often shown with hands folded in prayer or with a right hand extended to indicate guardianship of humans or God's protective love. The Christmas (herald) angels symbolize God's redeeming love; angels shown with trumpets suggest praise of God or proclamation of his name. They are used as symbols of the Last Day.

APPLE: Represents the fall of man and the Virgin. It also symbolizes man's temptation or attraction to the material world.

ARK: An ark floating upon the stormy waters symbolizes the church riding in safety amidst the world's struggles and tribulations. It shelters the faithful from the flood.

BELL: Represents a call to worship. It also signifies the preacher, who like a bell, encourages the faithful.

BOOK: The Bible, symbolic of authoritative wisdom or learning. An open book represents a relevant prophecy or saying.

BREAD & CHALICE: Symbols of Holy Communion. As a symbol of the body of Christ, bread is the source of man's redemption. In sharing the bread, the communicants become one in and with the body of Christ. The chalice or up holds the wine, or the blood or Christ.

BUTTERFLY: A symbol of the resurrection and eternal life. The three stages of the butterfly-caterpillar, larva, and butterfly - parallel terrestrial life, death, and final celestial destination.

CANDLE: Symbolizes Christ as the "Light of the World" and humans' aspiration for the source of all light and life. The number of candles also has significance:

ONE: Unity;

TWO: The dual natures of Christ—human and divine;

THREE: Holy Trinity;

FOUR: Advent;

FIVE: Five wounds of Christ;

SEVEN: The seven gifts of the Spirit, the Seven Sacraments.

CHRISTMAS TREE: Because the tree remains green throughout the winter when most plants die, the evergreens remain a symbol of life. The tree symbolizes the Garden of Eden's "Tree of Life" also the star on the Christmas tree reminds us of the star of Bethlehem; "the Light of the World."

CHURCH: Because Christians found refuge in the church, the ship became an early symbol for the church. The steeple or spire points heavenward. The steps or stairs at the entrance symbolize the pathway to God's ways. The large open doors of the church invite all people inside.

CROWN: The crown reminds us of Christ's victory over sin and death. It is a symbol of the divine nature of Jesus Christ.

CRUCIFIX: Not a symbol, but a representation of Christ suspended on the cross.

DOVE: A descending dove is probably the most universal symbol of the Holy Spirit. A dove with an olive branch symbolizes peace from the reconciliation between God and man. The dove with a drop of water symbolizes God using earthly water and divine spirit, to create life out of chaos. A dove with flames is symbolic of the fire of the Holy Spirit at Pentecost. Seven flames represent the seven gifts of the spirit.

EMMANUEL: This word is combination of three Hebrew words which mean "God with us."

FIRE/FLAME: Next to the dove, this is the most common symbol of the Holy Spirit. It represents destruction and regeneration, such as the "flames of Hell" or the "tongues of fire" associated with the Holy Spirit. It also represents Jesus as the "Light of the World." Seven flames refer to the seven gifts of the spirit.

FISH: Used in times of persecution as a secret sign by which Christians identified themselves to other Christians. The Greek word for fish formed an acrostic of the Greek phrase "Jesus Christ, God's Son, Savior." The symbol provided protection from non-Christians, and when drawn on the walls of underground passageways directed worshippers to meeting places. A single fish represent the Savior while several fishes represent faithful Christians.

FOLDED HANDS: Symbolic of prayer.

GREENERY: Used as a symbol of eternal life.

HAND OF GOD: When the hand of God proceeds from the clouds, a triradiant nimbus usually surrounds it. It is suggestive of the presence and sympathy of the Holy Trinity.

HEART: Reminds God's love for his people and the love of Christians for one another. The "Sacred Heart of Jesus" is symbolized by a heart pierced with three nails and encircled by the crown of thorns. A heart pierced by a sword symbolizes the Virgin Mary.

HOLLY: The thorns of the holly leaves symbolize the suffering of Jesus on the cross.

HOSANNA: The Greek form of the Hebrew petition "Save, we beseech Thee."

KEY: The key symbolizes the keys to the kingdom of heaven.

LAMB OF GOD: Or Agnus Dei, one of the oldest symbols known to the church. The banner shows us Jesus victorious over death. Sometimes the symbol is pictured on a book with seven seals. Other times, with four rivers for the Gospel flowing from four books.

LAMP/LANTERN: Symbolizes wisdom or knowledge. It is also a symbol of Christ. As stated in Psalms 119:105, "Thy word is a lamp unto my feet, and a light unto my path."

LILY: A symbol of the Virgin Mary and the state of purity and chastity attributed to her. It reminds us that Jesus was born without sin of a virgin.

MANGER: The manger, which is a feeding trough, has become a symbol of our Lord's nativity. Sometimes empty, or sometimes with the Holy Child in it. A nimbus surrounds his head.

NATIVITY: From the Latin word for cloud, it is a circle of light surrounding the head of saint. It is not a halo. Sometimes shown with three rays from the center (triradiant). A symbol of serenity or great distinction in the church, the rayed nimbus should be used only to symbolize God or a person of the Holy Trinity.

NOEL: From the Latin word natalis, which means "relating to birth". It now refers to the birth of Christ, or the Christmas season.

PALM BRANCH: Symbolizes triumph and victory over death and Christ's entry into Jerusalem. It is also a symbol of martyrdom.

RAINBOW: Symbolizes a reconciliation between God and man. God set it in the heavens as a promise floods will never come again.

ROSE: A symbol of the Messiah, Jesus' mother Mary and Christ's human birth and humility. The red rose that sprang from Christ's blood shed on Calvary, represents love and martyrdom.

SHELL: The scallop shell has become the symbol of baptism and pilgrimage. The shell and water united remind us of our birth as God's children through baptism,

SHIP: Symbolic of the church under the leadership of Christ. The church is the vessel of spiritual guidance for sailing over the sea or waters of life.

STAR:	Symbol of the divine light. The star shining in the night represents the Holy Spirit penetrating the darkness. The nativity star heralds the birth of Christ, the bright morning star.

CROSS STAR: A four point star.

BETHLEHEM STAR: A five point star (Epiphany Star, Star of Jessie)

CREATOR'S STAR: A six point star, symbolic of the six days of creation (Star of David).

MYSTIC STAR: A seven point star. Represents the seven gifts of the Holy Spirit.

STAR OF REGENERATION: An eight point star (star of baptism).

FRUITS OF THE SPIRIT STAR: A nine point star.

STAR OF THE APOSTLES: A twelve point star (star of the twelve tribes).

STEEPLE: Pointing upward, where Christ sits at the right hand of God the Father.

SUN: It is masculine, as opposed to the moon, which is feminine. A sign of the joy and hope that dispels the darkness and despair of sin, the son symbolizes Christ's resurrection.

SWORD: The symbol of power and authority, it is linked to the cross by its shape.

TORCH: The torch signifies Christian witnessing. "Let your light so shine before men, that they may see your good works, and glorify your Father which is in heaven" (Matthew 5:16).

TREE: As a counterpart to the ladder and the pillar, the tree is symbolic of the link between heaven and earth. The tree's three main divisions (roots, trunk and branches) also correspond to the three divisions of man (body, mind, and spirit).

WATER: A symbol of holy baptism. It is a source of life. It is also symbolic of an inner or higher truth, rather than the outer literal significance of the rock.

WHALE: Symbolic of the tomb from which men will emerge, overcoming death to have eternal life.

WINDOW: The window is inseparable from the symbolism of light.

SYMBOLISM OF COLOR

Colors also symbolically speak of the Christian faith.

For those interested in painting any portion of their design, the following provides information on color variation and its meaning.

( ) - Denotes traditional associations with the Western world.

BLACK: Denotes mourning, grief, sorrow, death and remembrance. (sin, death, evil)

BLUE: Suggests good health, eternity, and heaven. (hope, love, truth, faithfulness, heaven)

BROWN: The color of the earth, happiness.

GREEN: Green is the universal color of nature. It is also the color of life, growth, innocence, freshness,and a symbol for the Holy Trinity. (growth, victory, hope)

ORANGE: Ambition, endurance.

PURPLE: Ancient color of royalty. Faith, trust, penitence. It is equally appropriate to be used in lieu of violet.

RED: A color for the Holy Spirit. It represents humanity, love, bravery, and trust. It also refers to the blood of the martyrs of the church. (fire, love)

ROYAL BLUE: Trust.

SCARLET: (royalty, loyalty).

VIOLET: Suggests penitence, sorrow, humility, suffering, sympathy, and fasting. (royalty, repentance, remorse).

WHITE: Symbolic of gladness, glory, light, joy, and purity. White is the color of the Creator (purity, holiness, innocence, faith, light).

YELLOW/GOLD: Represents the glory of God and the might of his people, wisdom. (gold: God's abundance, marriage).

CHURCH CALENDAR COLORS: Certain colors have become associated with the church year. Listed below are the major and minor church festivals and special occasions along with their symbolic color.

ADVENT: Violet or blue.

NEW YEAR'S EVE/DAY: White.

EPIPHANY: White (2nd through 8th Sundays—green).

TRANSFIGURATION OF OUR LORD: White.

ASH WEDNESDAY: Violet or black.

LENT: Violet.

PALM SUNDAY: Scarlet or violet.

MAUNDAY THURSDAY: Scarlet or white.

GOOD FRIDAY:	Black.
EASTER:	White (Easter Day—white or gold).
PENTECOST:	Red.
TRINITY SUNDAY:	White.
SEASON AFTER PENTECOST:	Green.
REFORMATION DAYS:	Red.
ALL SAINTS' DAY:	White.
THANKSGIVING DAY:	White.

MESSAGE THROUGH DESIGN

Although many of the designs in this book are self-explanatory, some designs incorporate several symbols to convey a special meaning. Some of the designs included in this book are listed below along with the intended messages.

WEDDING AND ANNIVERSARIES: The two banded rings in these designs symbolize the couple being united into one flesh. The linked rings show that Christ binds the couple together in love.

When these banded rings are intertwined in a symbol for Christ, such as cross, Chi Rho, dove, circle, or Cross of Constantine, the rings become symbolic of a desire to have Christ as the center of the couple's life together.

The cross represents the union of opposites and reminds of the ultimate sacrificial love. The dove represents the presence of God through the Holy Spirit. The heart symbolizes the promise a couple makes before God. The butterfly is symbolic of the couple's beginning a new life together through Christian marriage while the plant represents the believers who know that new life begins in Christ. The circle is used in these designs to suggest unity and eternity.

BAPTISM IN CHRIST: The shell and water united together symbolize the sacrament of baptism. The dove represents meekness, purity, and the splendor of righteousness and is symbolic of the Holy Spirit. Three drops of water are used to remind us that the ceremony is done in the name of the Father, the Son, and the Holy Spirit.

LAMB OF GOD: The halo around the lamb distinguishes it as the "Lamb of God," who was sacrificed on the cross for the forgiveness of sins.

CHURCH ON A ROCK: According to Matthew 16:18, ". . . and upon this rock I will build my church; and the gates of Hell shall not prevail against it." Those who hear the words of God and does them, will be like the wise man who built his house upon a rock, a secure foundation.

CHRIST WITH OPEN ARMS: All people are welcomed to accept salvation through faith in Christ.

CROSS/CHALICE/BREAD: The bread and wine (chalice) symbolize the body and blood of Christ, shed on the cross for the forgiveness of sins.

CHALICE/BREAD/CANDLE: The bread and wine (the body and blood of Christ) are united together in communion for the forgiveness of sins and renewed strength in faith.

STAR/CROSS/CROWN/MANGER: The star's rays descend to form the manger. The newborn king and those who came to worship him are represented by the crown which is above the manger.

EPHIPHANY CHI RHO: The first two letters of Christ, in Greek, combined to form a symbol representing Christ's birth. A manger is formed with a nimbus above it.

ADVENT CANDLES: Symbolize the four Sundays of Advent. The cross, berries, and the thorns of the holy leaves remind us of Christ's suffering on the cross where he shed his blood for the forgiveness of sins.

This design makes a beautiful candle holder as pictured above. Other cross designs can also be substituted.

Cross of Constantine

Christ the Conquering King. This cross is the Chi Rho (explained later) except with the "X" turned to form the cross

A nice selection of jewelry, key rings and letter openers incorporating cross designs. See the letter openers chapter on page 124 for more designs.

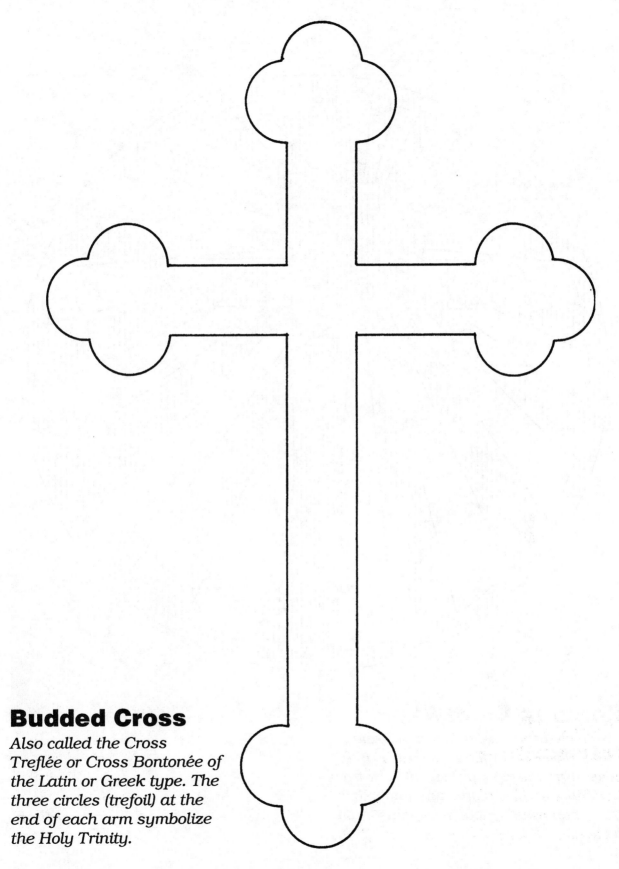

Budded Cross

Also called the Cross Treflée or Cross Bontonée of the Latin or Greek type. The three circles (trefoil) at the end of each arm symbolize the Holy Trinity.

3

Cross in Glory #1

Also called the Easter Cross or Rayed Cross. The Latin type cross has Easter lilies surrounding it or rays of light from a rising sun. The rising sun symbolizes the conquering of death by Jesus' resurrection.

4

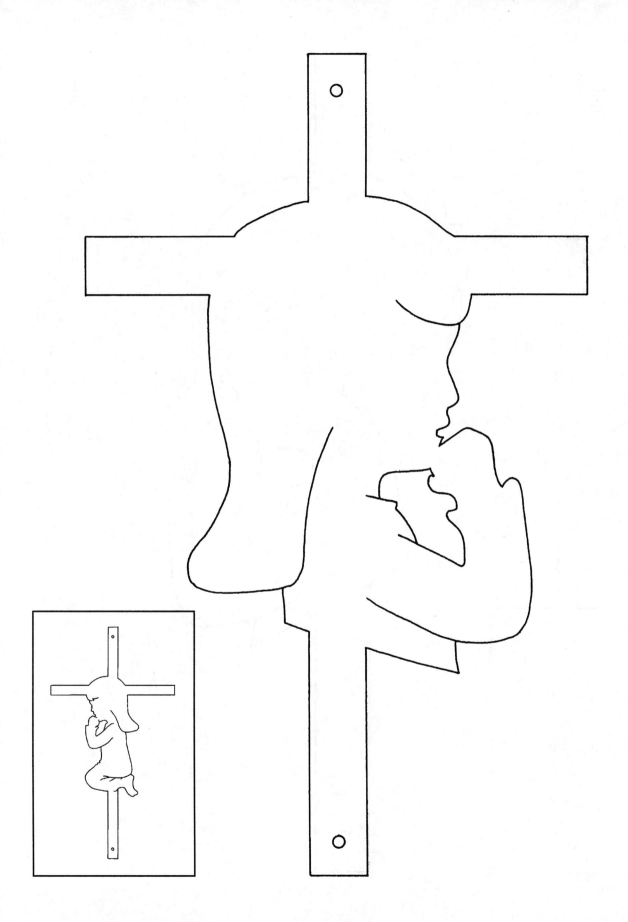

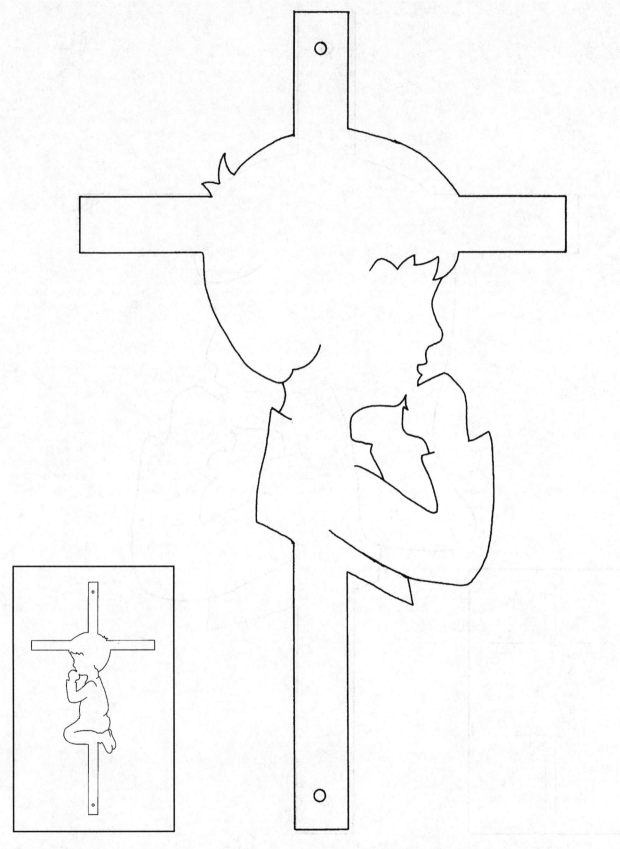

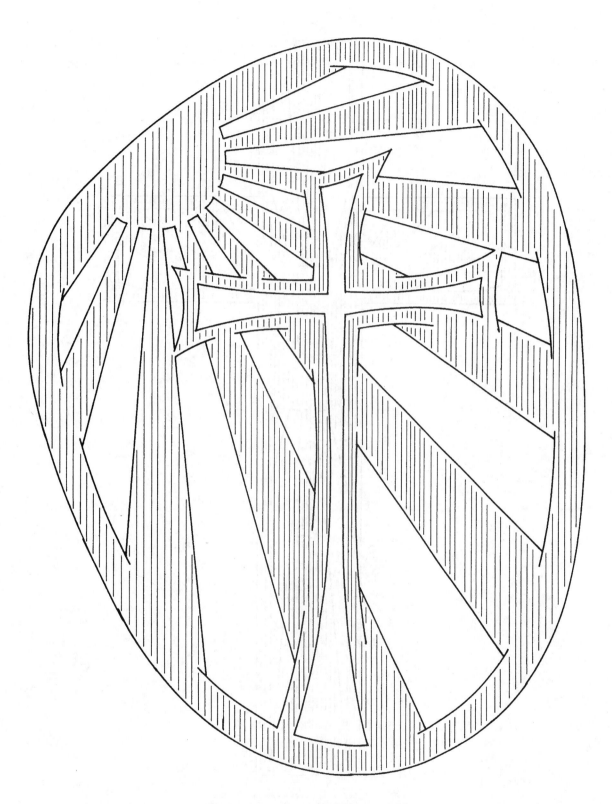

Cross in Glory #2

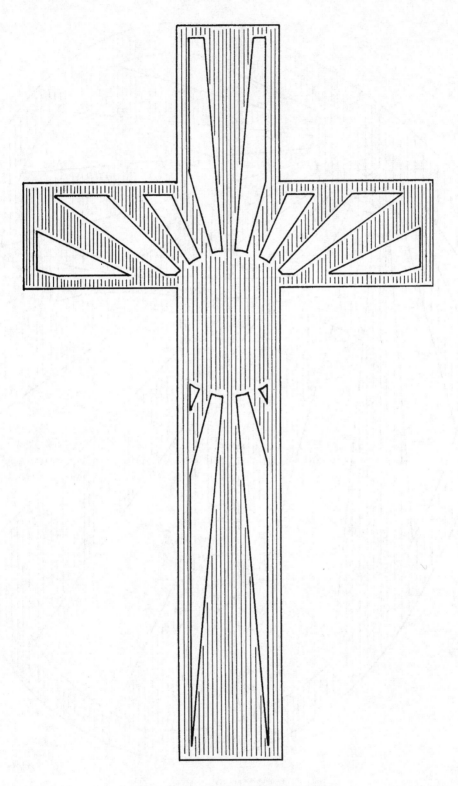

Cross in Glory #3

**Cross in
Glory: Lily**

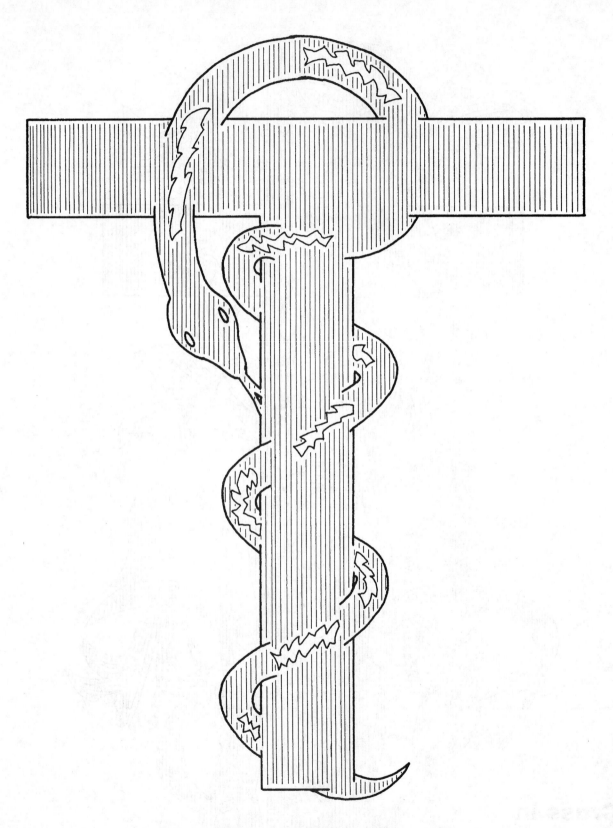

Tau Cross With Serpent

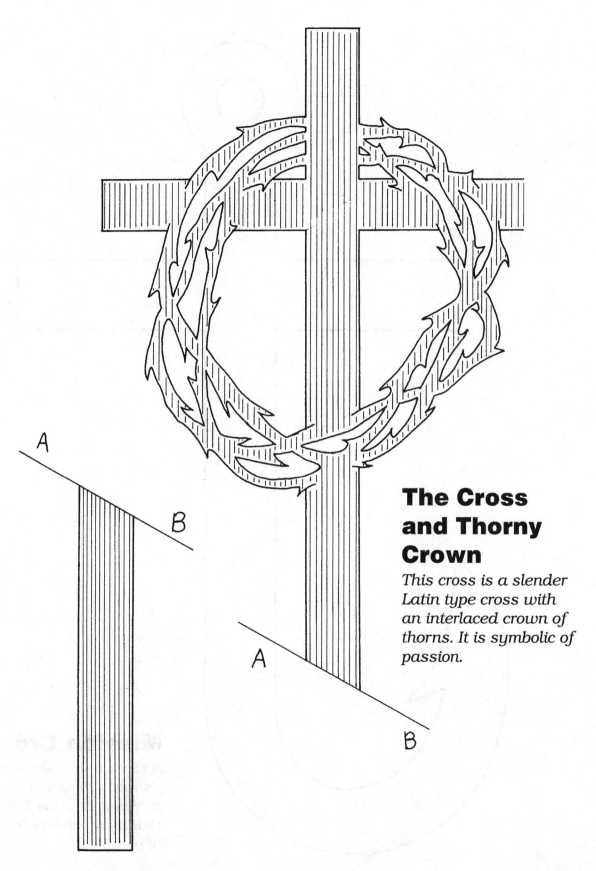

The Cross and Thorny Crown

This cross is a slender Latin type cross with an interlaced crown of thorns. It is symbolic of passion.

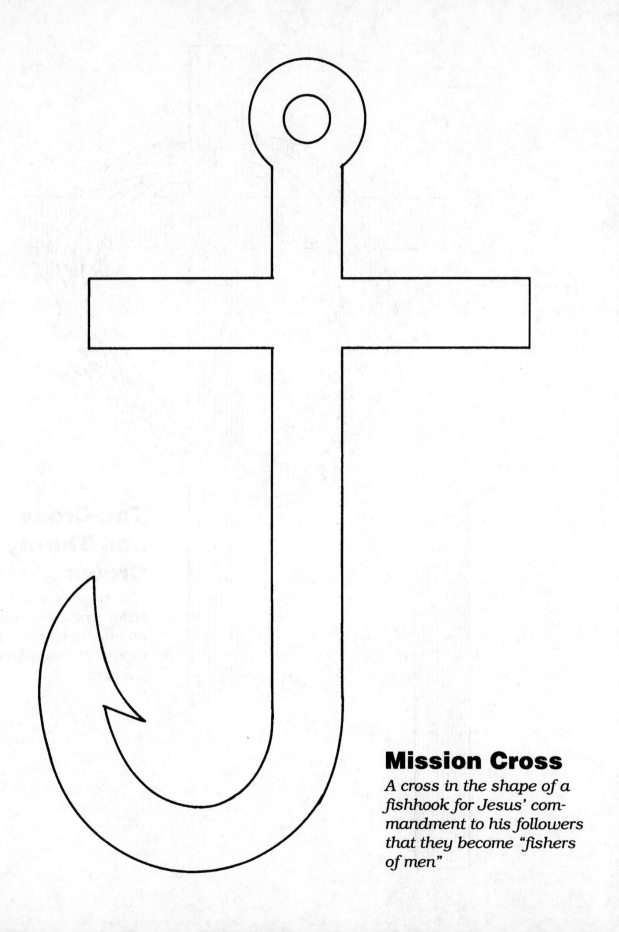

Mission Cross

A cross in the shape of a fishhook for Jesus' commandment to his followers that they become "fishers of men"

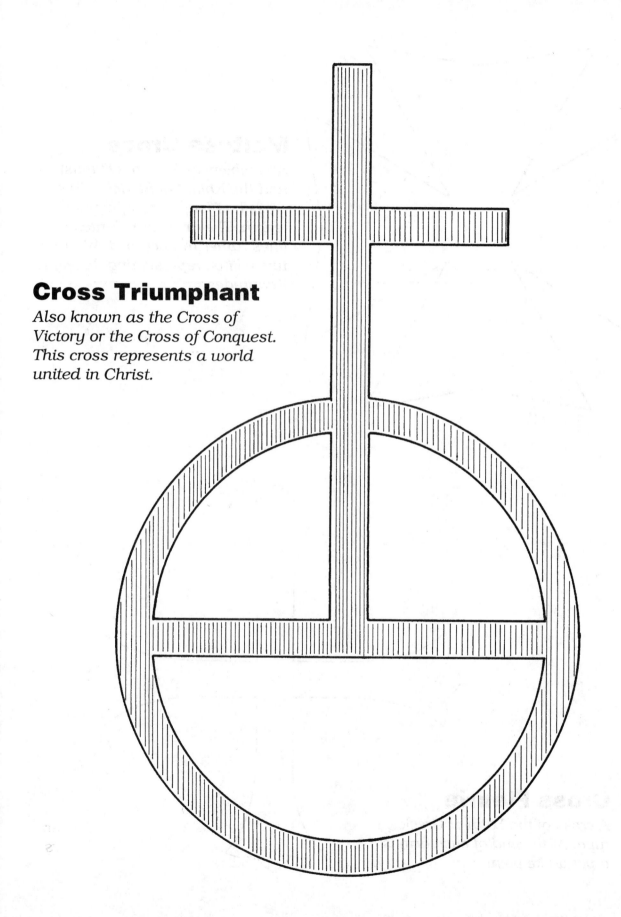

Cross Triumphant

Also known as the Cross of Victory or the Cross of Conquest. This cross represents a world united in Christ.

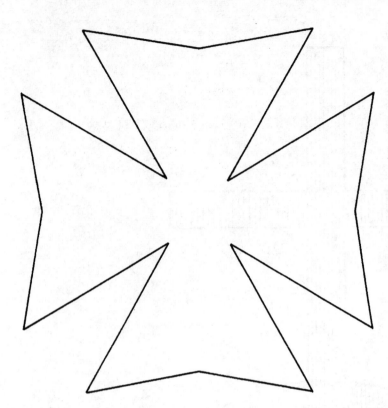

Maltese Cross

An emblem of John the Baptist and the Knight of St. John. The cross has four arms of equal length. The arms are slanted lines rather than curved. With two points, representing the eight Beatitudes.

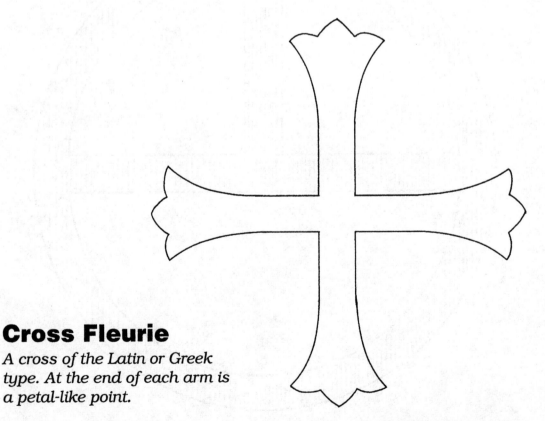

Cross Fleurie

A cross of the Latin or Greek type. At the end of each arm is a petal-like point.

Cross
Fleur-de-Lis
At the end of each large arm is a fleur-de-lis.

Trinity Cross
Similar to the Cross Fleur-de-lis, but much more intricate and beautiful. At the end of each arm are three fleur-de-lis.

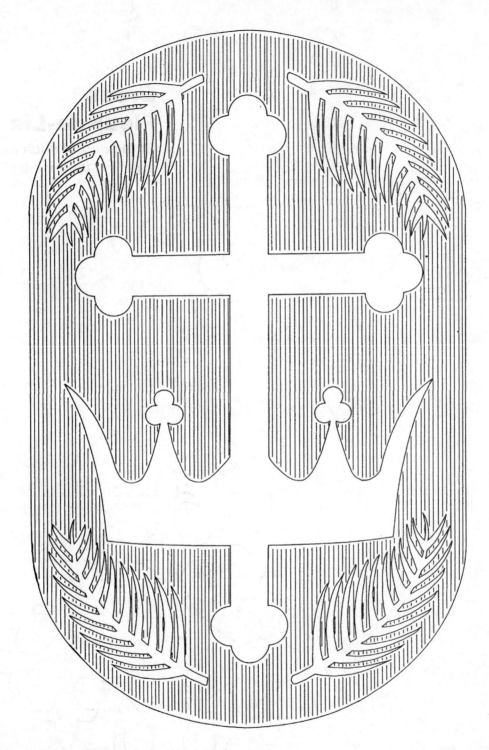

Cross and Crown

Symbolizes a reward to those who are faithful unto death. Palm branches surround the cross and crown, reminding of Jesus' triumphant entry into Jerusalem.

Shepherd's Crook Cross

The shepherd's crook, Symbolizes Jesus as the Good Shepherd,. This cross reminds us of who laid down his life for the sheep.

17

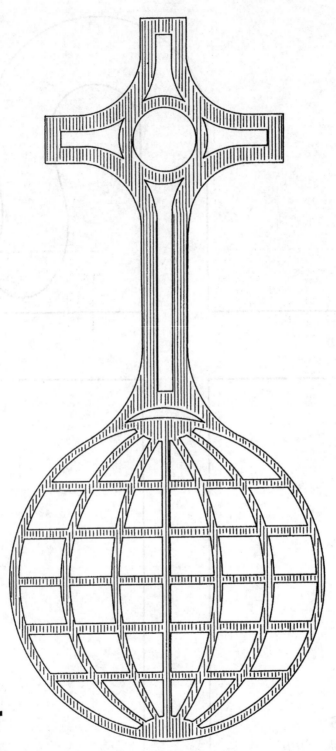

Cross Over the World

A cross reigns over the world, represented by the ball. This cross symbolizes the triumph of Jesus over the sins of the world.

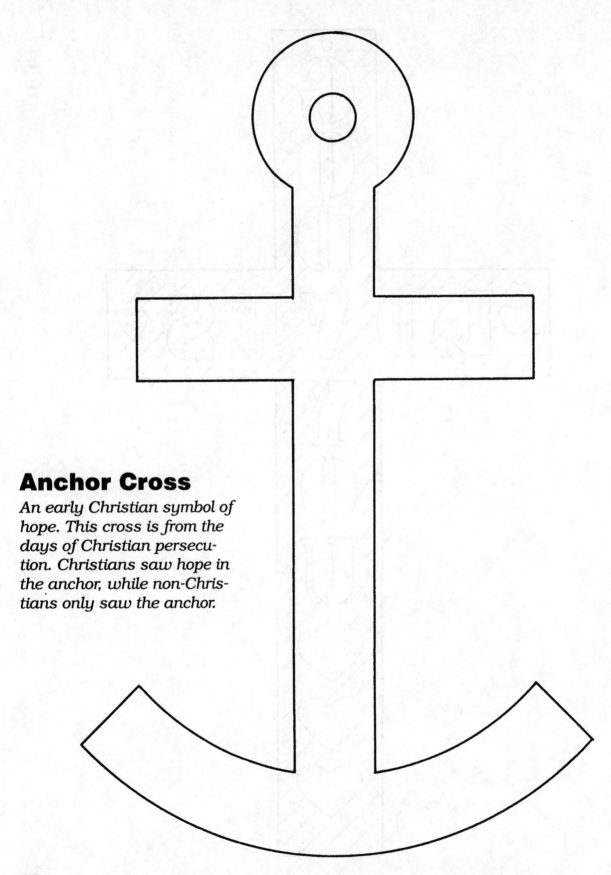

Anchor Cross

An early Christian symbol of hope. This cross is from the days of Christian persecution. Christians saw hope in the anchor, while non-Christians only saw the anchor.

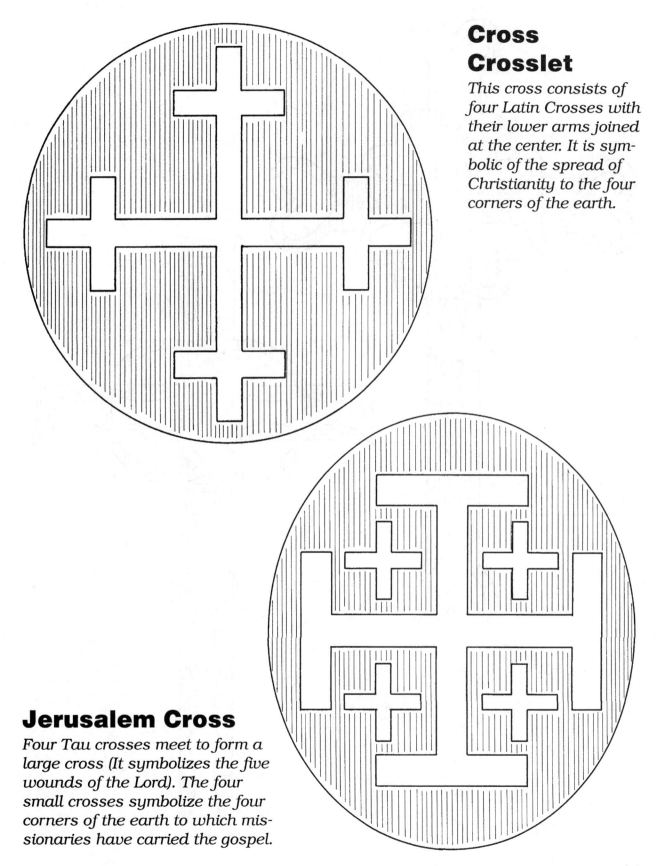

Cross Crosslet

This cross consists of four Latin Crosses with their lower arms joined at the center. It is symbolic of the spread of Christianity to the four corners of the earth.

Jerusalem Cross

Four Tau crosses meet to form a large cross (It symbolizes the five wounds of the Lord). The four small crosses symbolize the four corners of the earth to which missionaries have carried the gospel.

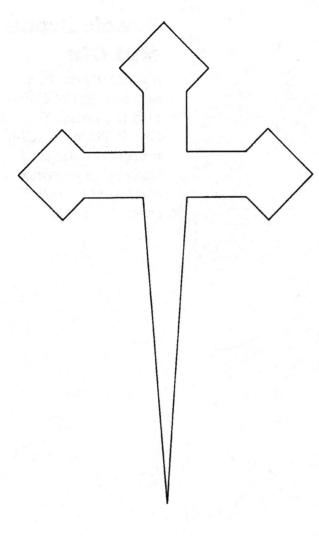

Cross Fitchey

Fitchey means to fix. The lower arm of the cross terminates in a point allowing the cross to be fixed (planted) in the ground The origin of this cross is presumed to be from the practice of taking an oath on the handle of a sword which forms a cross with the blade.

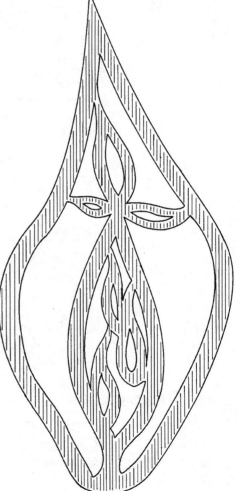

Firey Cross

Also known as the Cross Flamant. The flames symbolize the intensity and passion of one filled with the Holy Spirit.

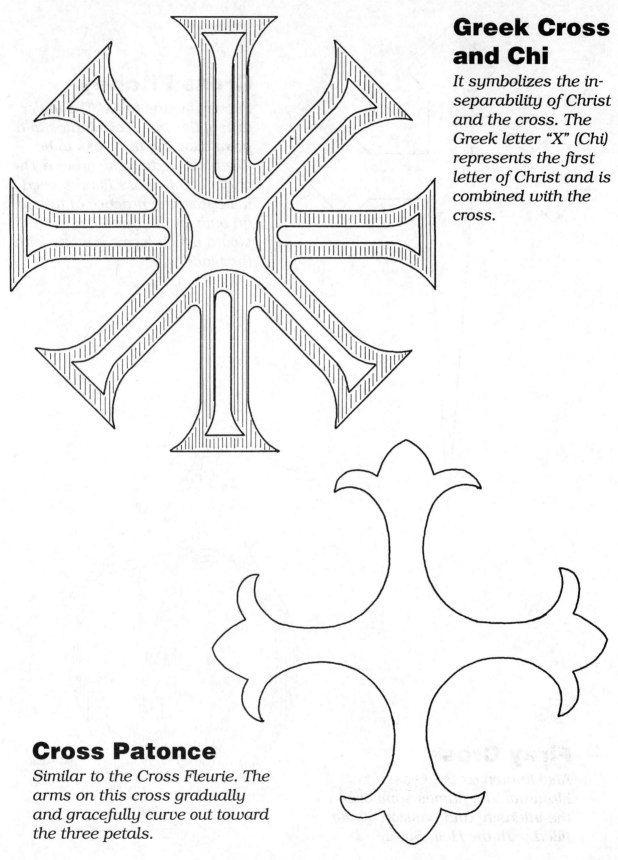

Greek Cross and Chi

It symbolizes the inseparability of Christ and the cross. The Greek letter "X" (Chi) represents the first letter of Christ and is combined with the cross.

Cross Patonce

Similar to the Cross Fleurie. The arms on this cross gradually and gracefully curve out toward the three petals.

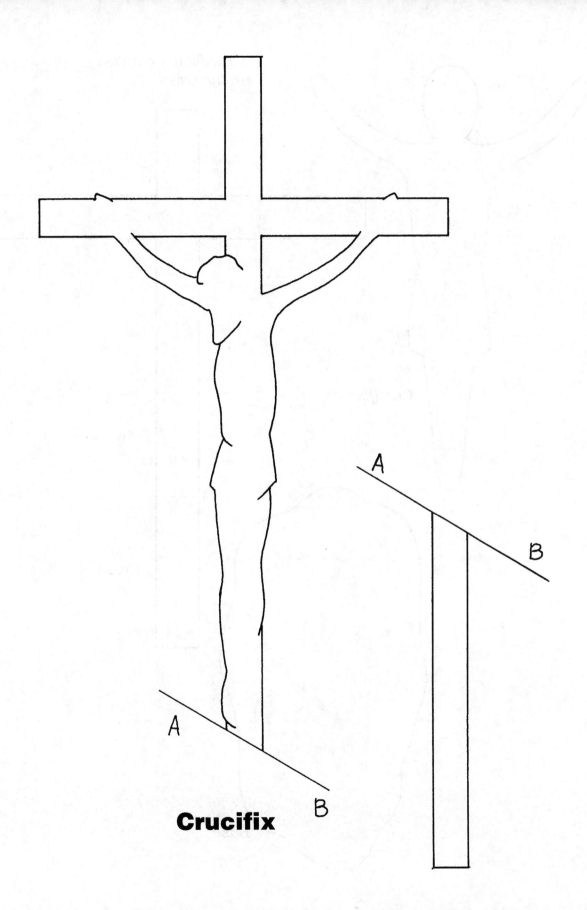

Crucifix

27

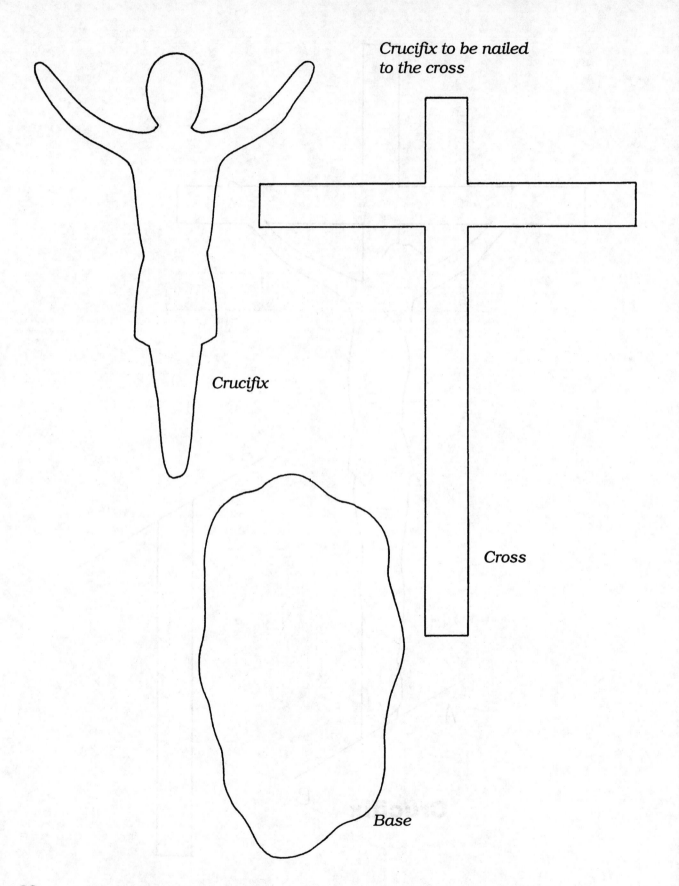

Crucifix to be nailed
to the cross

Crucifix

Cross

Base

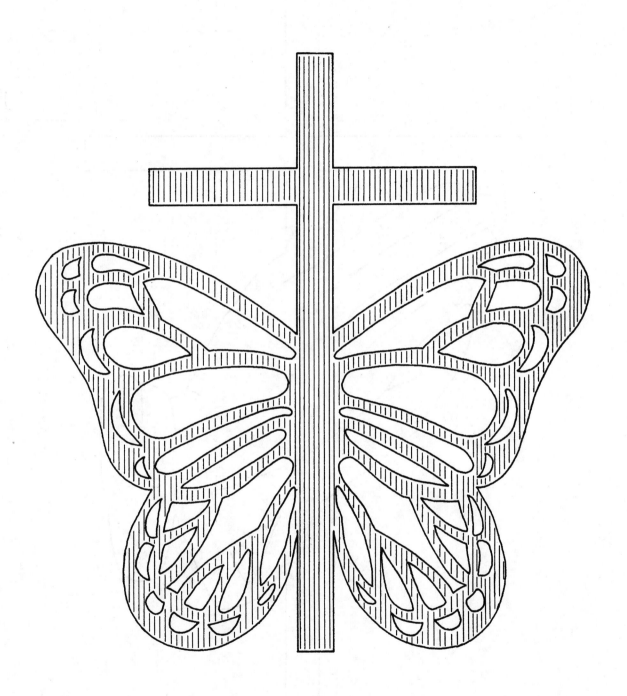

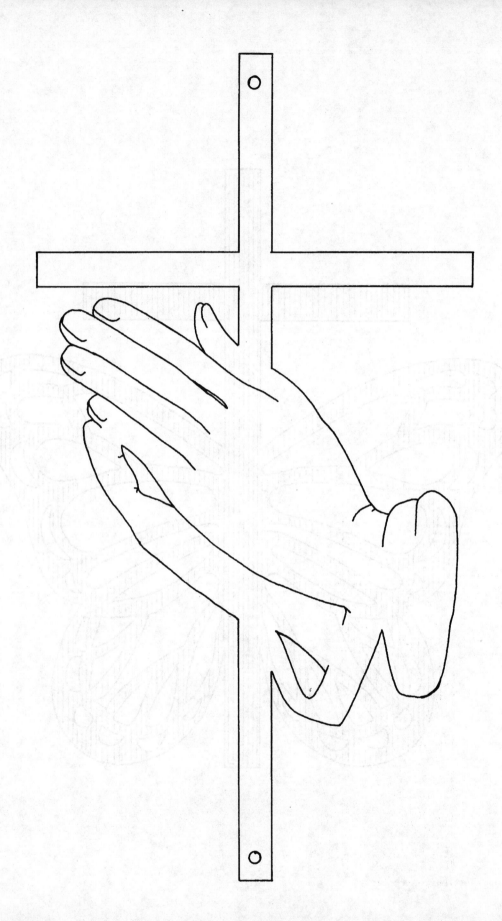

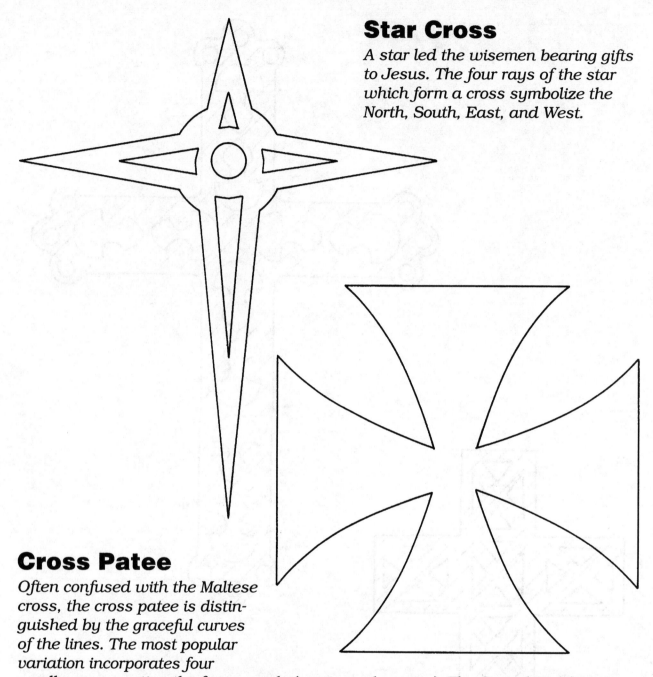

Star Cross

A star led the wisemen bearing gifts to Jesus. The four rays of the star which form a cross symbolize the North, South, East, and West.

Cross Patee

Often confused with the Maltese cross, the cross patee is distinguished by the graceful curves of the lines. The most popular variation incorporates four scrolls, representing the four gospels (one in each corner). The Gospel Matthew is represented by a winged man (stressing the Lord's human nature), Mark by a winged lion, Luke by a winged ox, and John by a winged eagle. The wings represent the divine inspiration of the four accounts of Jesus' time on earth. The scrolls should be positioned as follows:

Matthew - upper left
Mark - lower left
Luke - lower right
John - upper right

PLAQUES, SIGNS AND LETTERING

Matthew 28:20

John 8:12

John 11:25

John 14:6

37

John 15:5

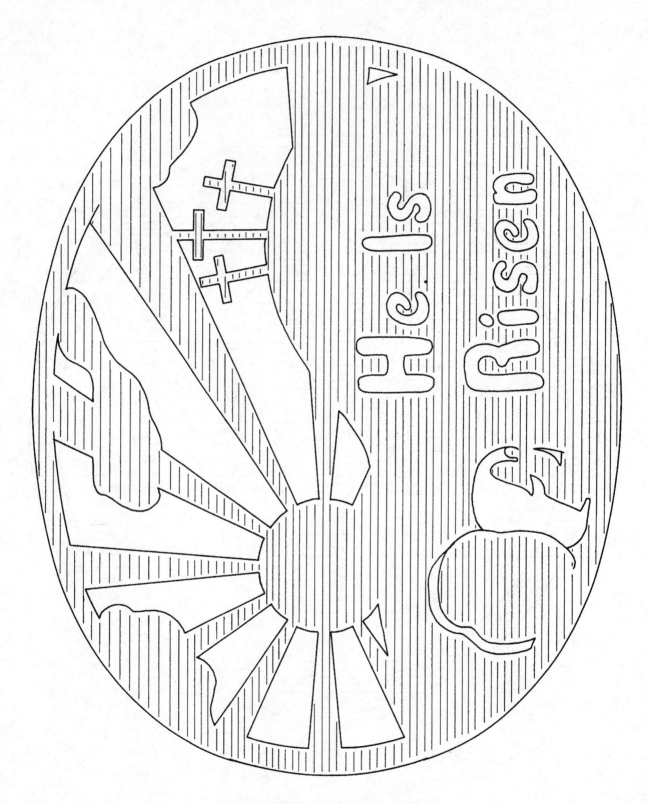

Matthew 28:6

41

44

48

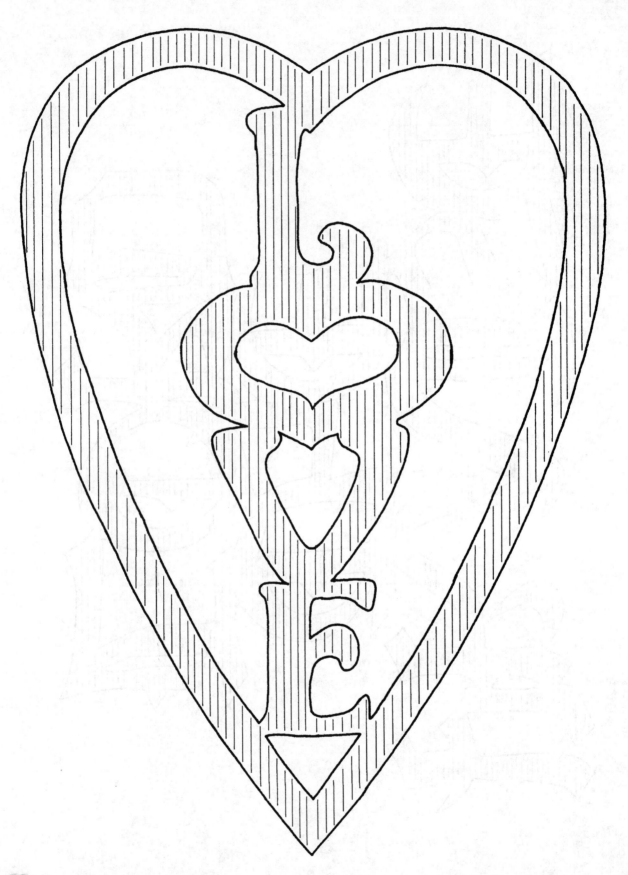

Ecclesiastes 3:1

ABCDEFGHI
JKLMNOPQR
STUVWXYZ&

1 2 3 4 5
6 7 8 9 0

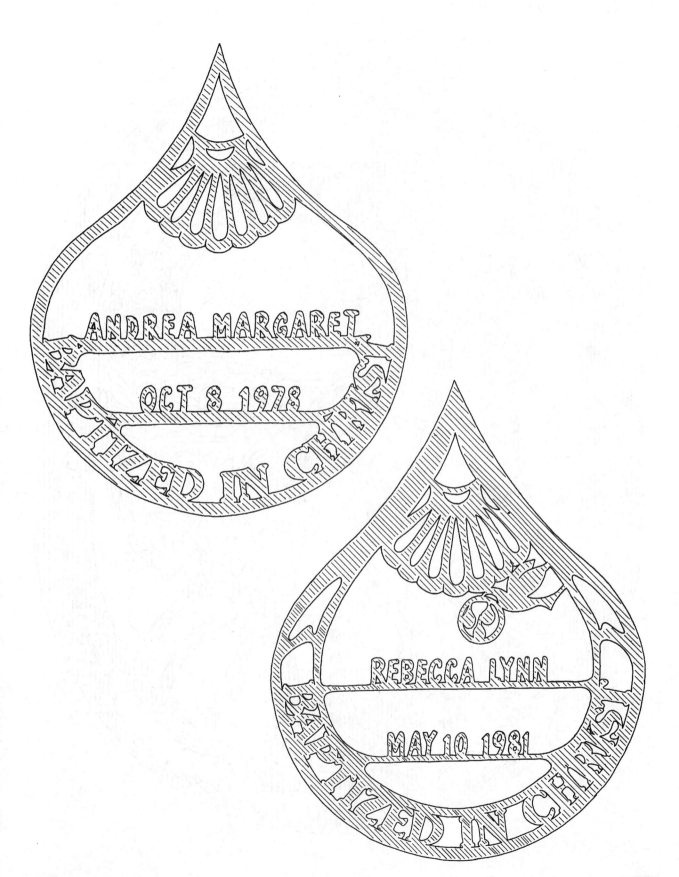

ANDREA MARGARET

OCT 8 1978

BAPTIZED IN CHRIST

REBECCA LYNN

MAY 10 1981

BAPTIZED IN CHRIST

56

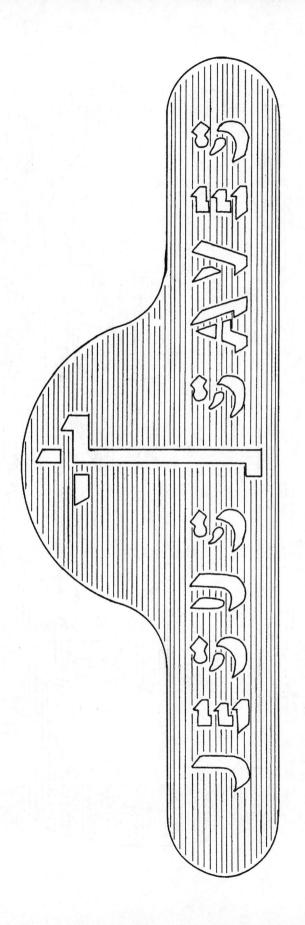

In All Things Give Thanks

63

This pattern can be cut from solid wood or from a platter blank as in the photo to the left.

CHRISTMAS

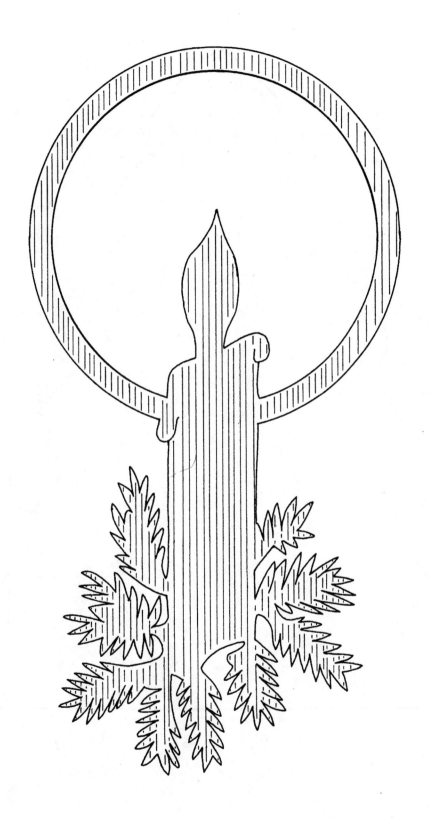

71

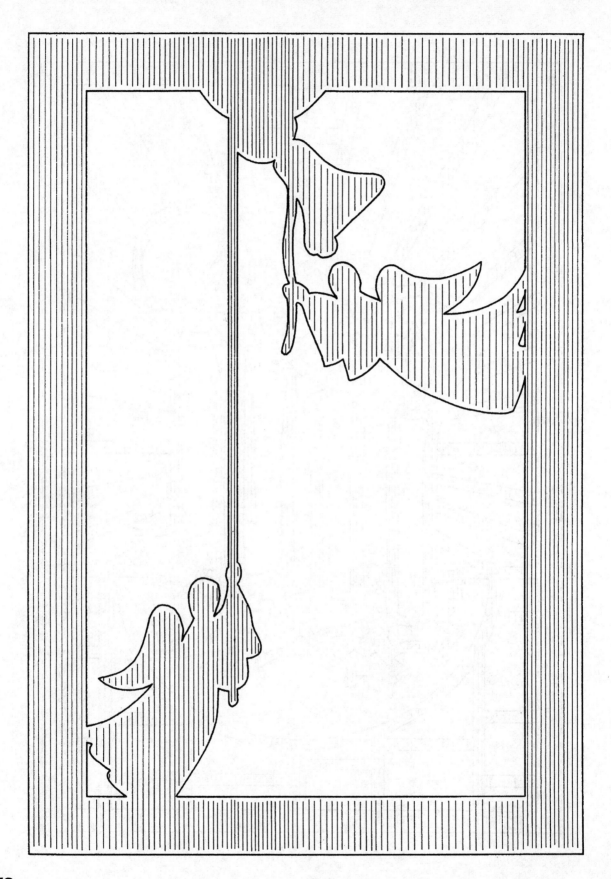

Nativity Set

This simple but classic Nativity scene contains 15 pieces found here on pages 73-77. Pieces can be left natural, strained or painted. Gold leaf or paint can be used to accent the star.

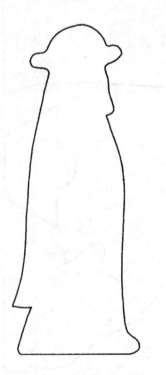

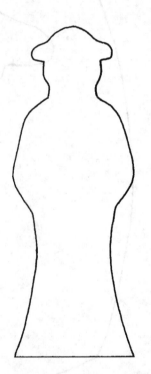

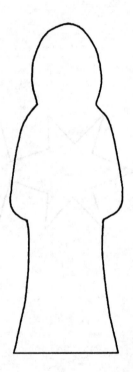

Shepherds

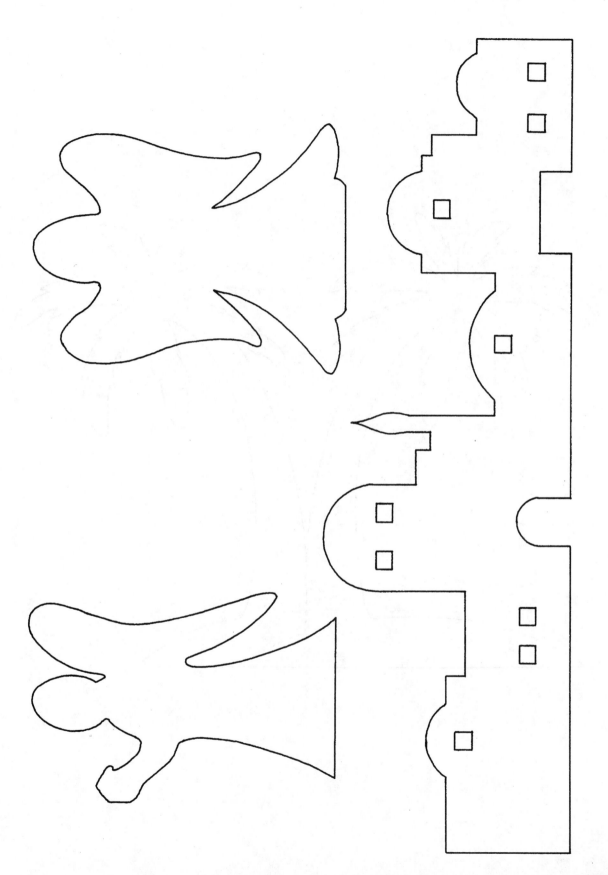

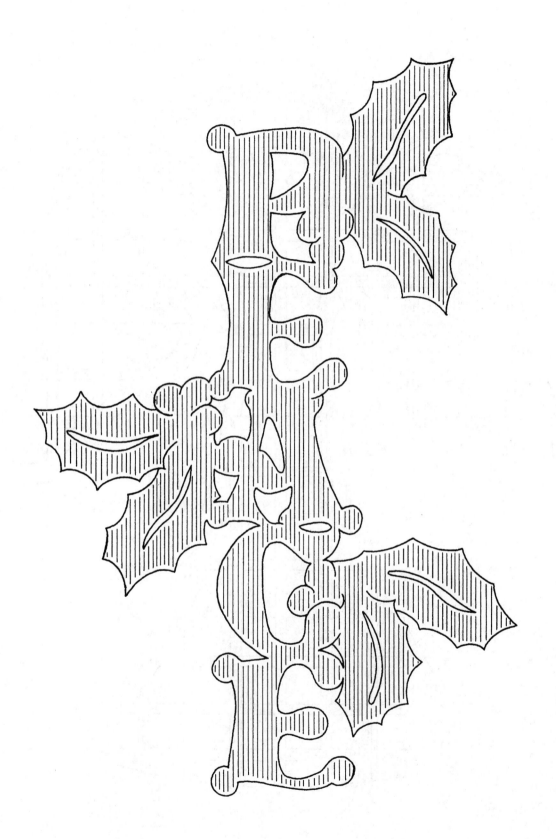

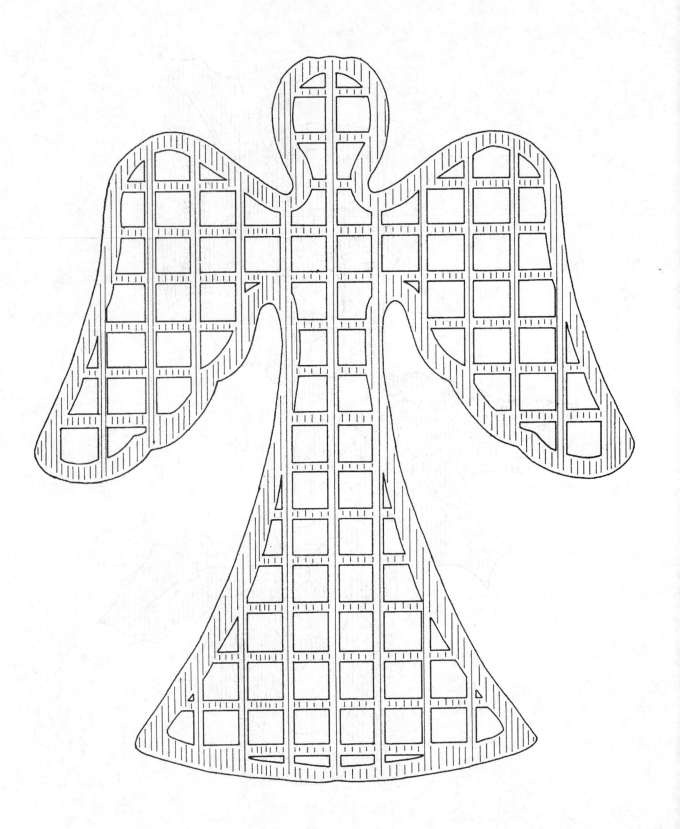

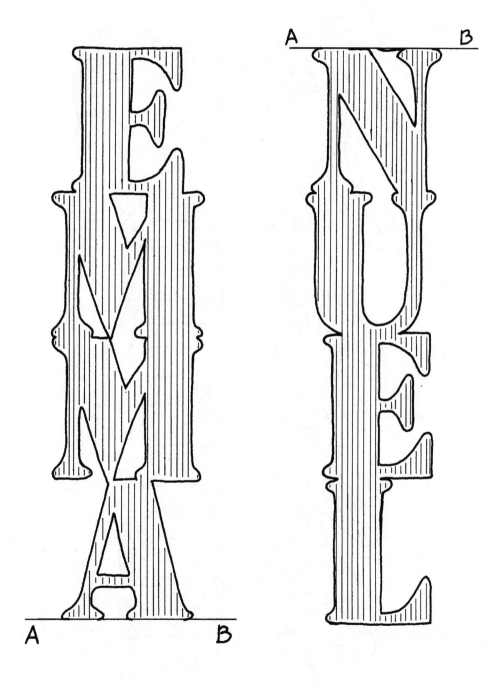

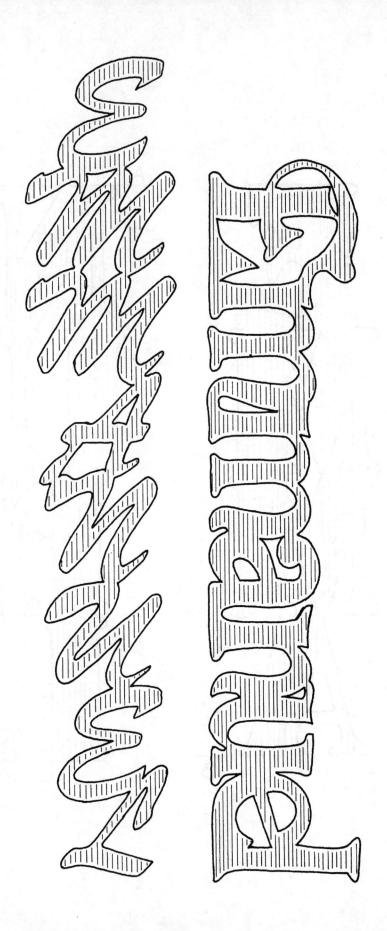

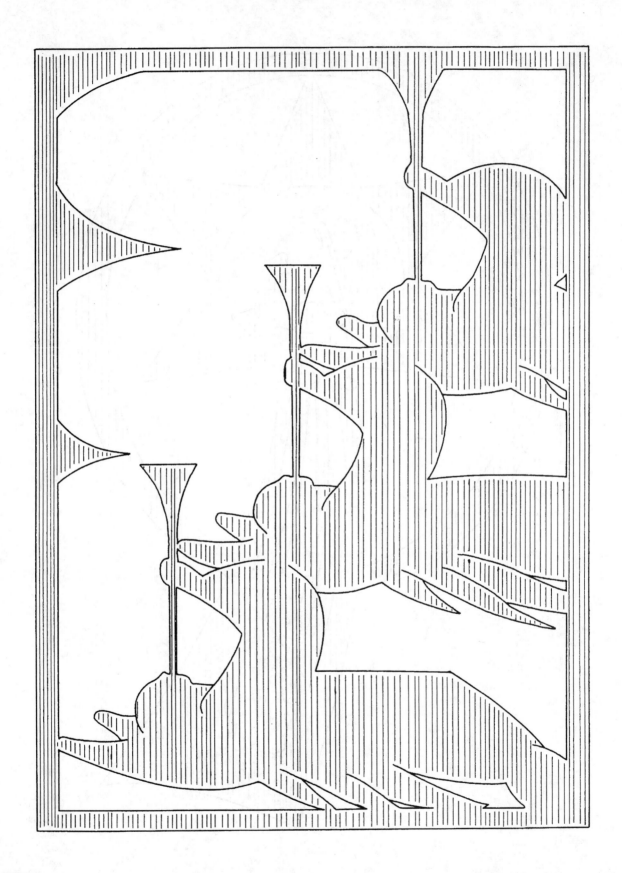

84

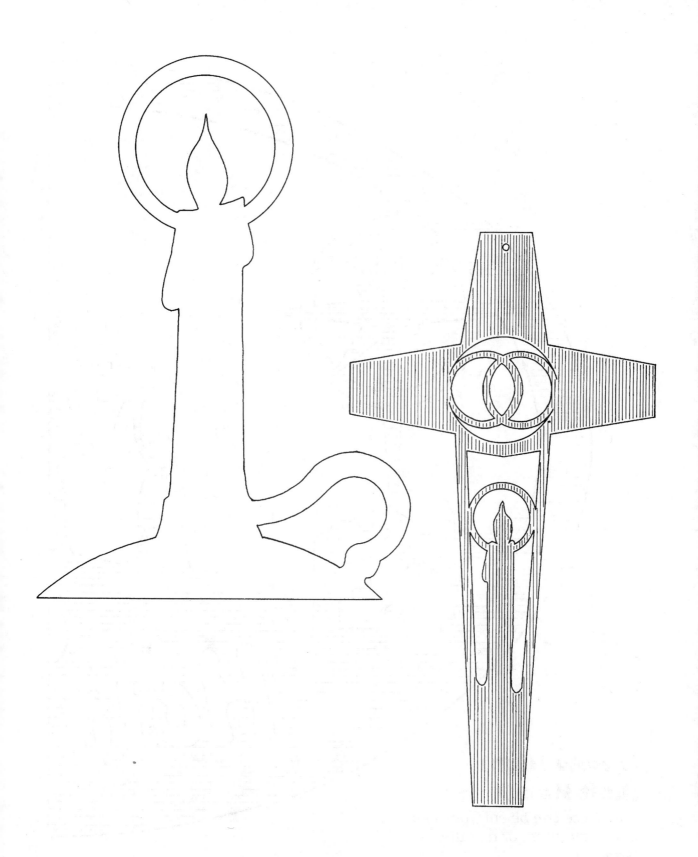

A

B

O Holy Night
(Left Hand)

This piece can be cut from solid wood, plywood, or a platter blank

**O Holy Night
(Right Hand)**

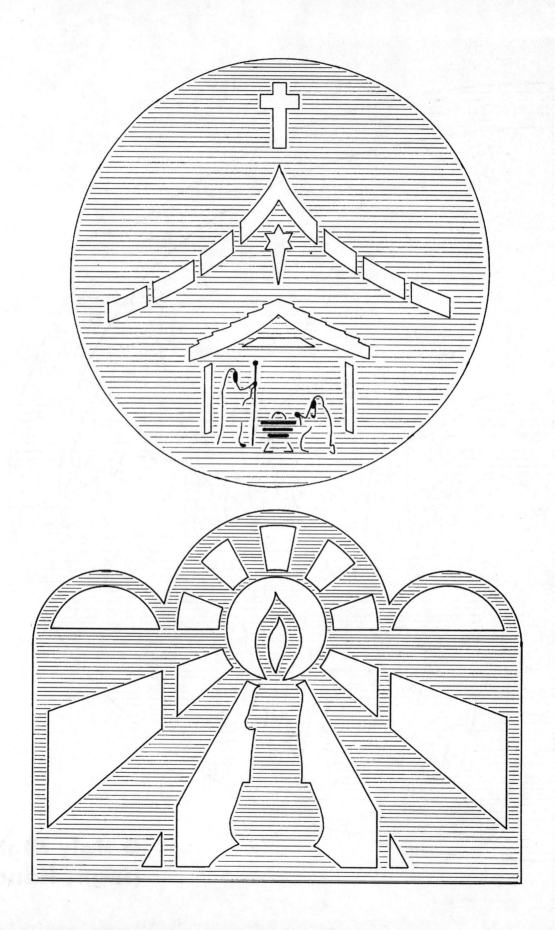

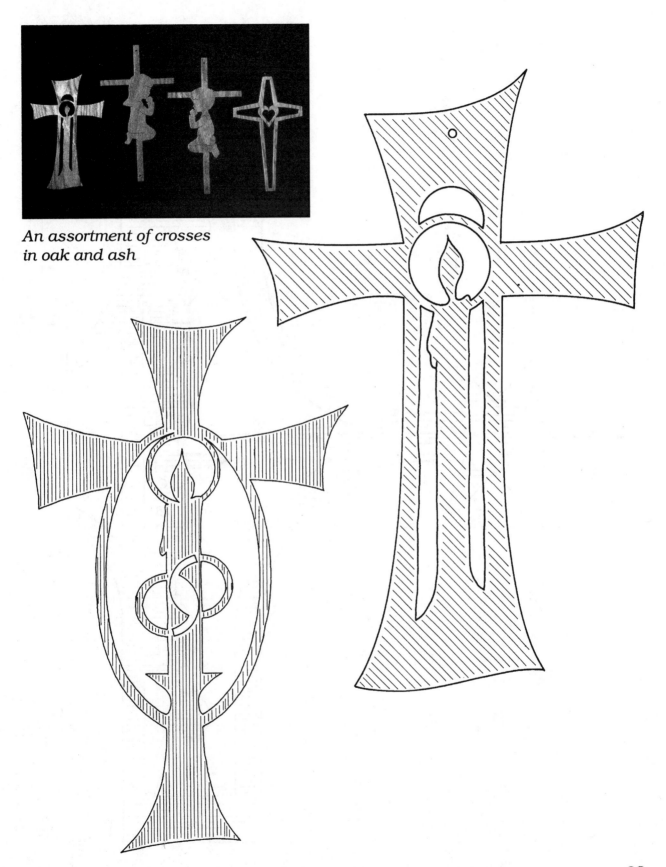

An assortment of crosses
in oak and ash

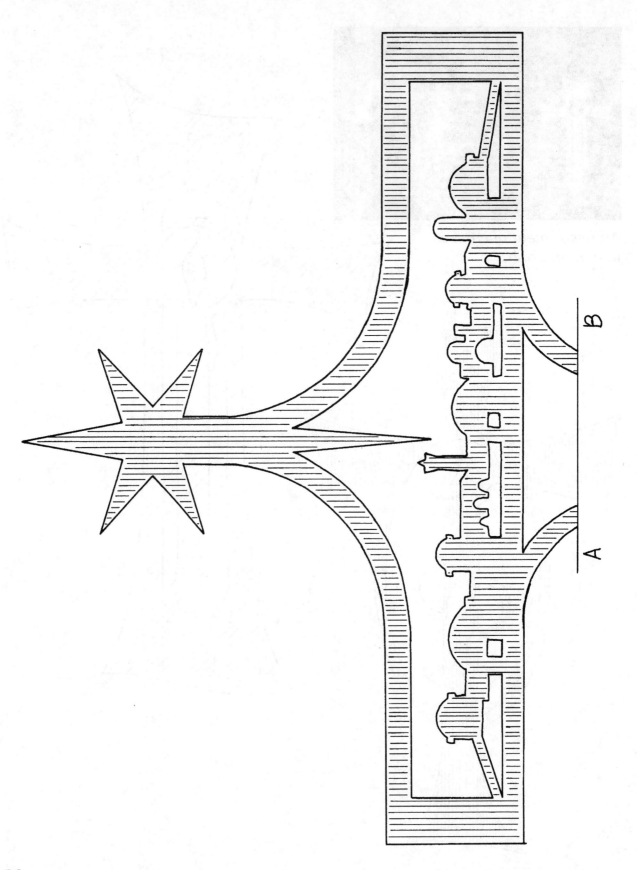

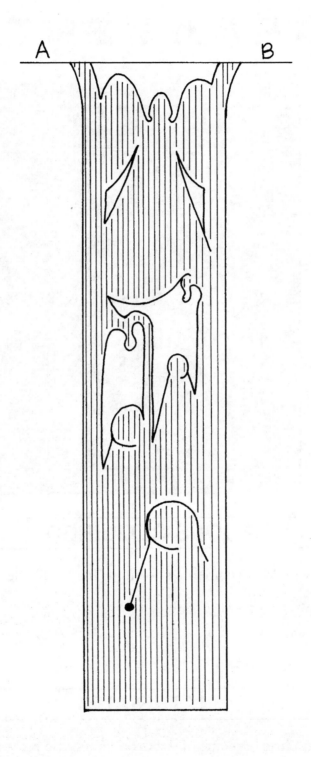

A   B

JIGSAW PUZZLE ORNAMENTS

TOOLS REQUIRED

To make the jigsaw puzzle ornaments shown in this book, the following tools will be needed:
- A scroll saw, coping saw, or fret saw;
- A drill press;
- A 3/32" drill bit.

MATERIALS

Because of the thin parts on some of the ornaments, the recommended wood is 3/8" thick plywood. However, 3/8" thick softwood or hardwood will also work.

CUTTING OUT THE ORNAMENTS

Trace the pattern onto the wood or make a photocopy and paste it to the wood with spray adhesive. Heavy solid black lines indicate the "cut lines".

To cut the ornaments out, a skiptooth blade will work well. Select a blade with 11.5 to 12.5 teeth per inch and a width and thickness of .043" x .016" or .037" x .015". Each ornament requires a 3/32" hole drilled down through the center. The center line is indicated by a dashed line on each pattern. Although some ornaments can be drilled prior to cutting, many will require cutting the ornament first. Then drill as far as the bit will allow, remove the drilled pieces, and then drill some more. A standard length bit will work find, but an extended length bit will allow for the maximum spindle travel of the drill press. Extended length drill bits are manufactured by the Donald E. Savard Company. A six inch (#38806) bit and a twelve inch (#38406) bit are available.

When making these ornaments or designing your own, remember the centerline must penetrate each individual piece of the ornament. All of the ornament pieces are held together by the string used for hanging the ornament.

Some of the ornaments require cutting sharp inside corners. Spin the workpiece around the blade to make these cuts. The best way to cut sharp corners is to stand directly in front of the saw and feed the material steadily into the blade. When a sharp turn is required reduce the feeding pressure while spinning the workpiece sharply around the blade. Do not put pressure sideways on the blade. When the patter lines up with the front of the blade, begin feeding the material again.

FINISHING

After cutting the ornaments out, sand the edges smooth with 100 grit sandpaper. Then sand the entire ornament with 220 grit sandpaper prior to painting. You may paint and decorate ornaments with acrylic colors.

A suitable string or cord loop (knotted at the bottom) has to be inserted through the hole to hang the ornament. An easy way to string the ornament is first to assemble all of the pieces. Then insert through the hole from the top to the bottom a fine piece of piano wire with a small hook bent on the end. Hook the top of the string loop and pull it up through the hole. A small amount of glue at the top of the hole will keep the string in place and prevent the ornament from falling apart.

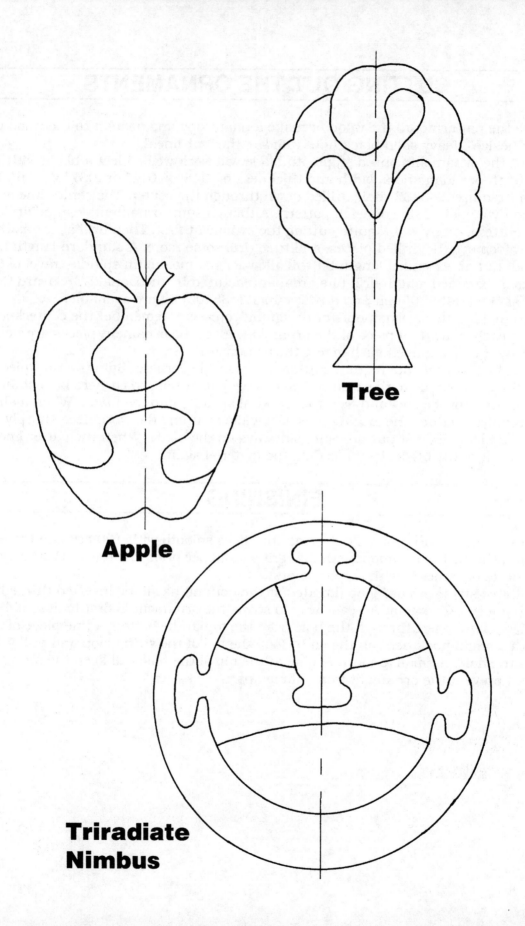

Tree

Apple

**Triradiate
Nimbus**

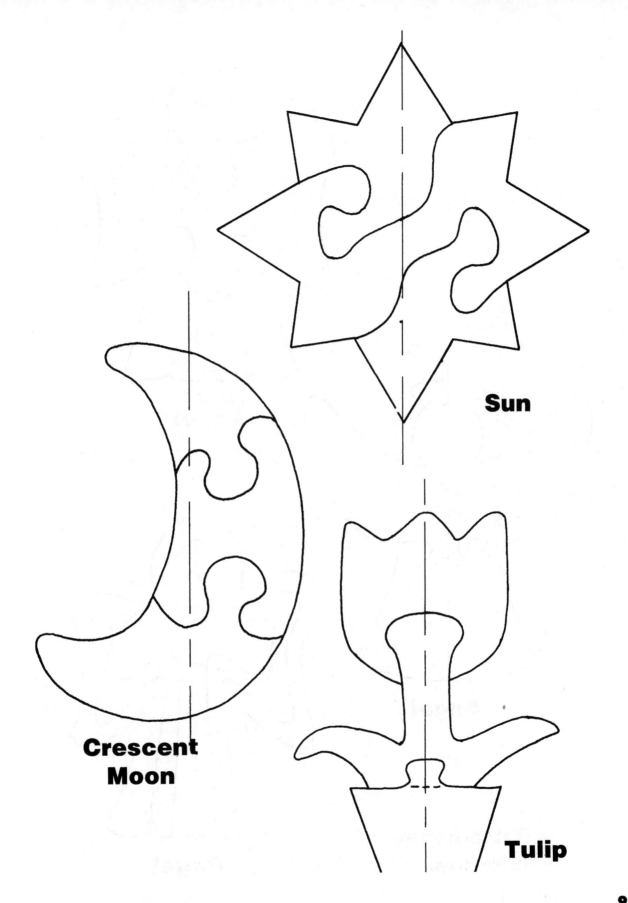

Sun

**Crescent
Moon**

Tulip

95

Angel

Angel

Angel

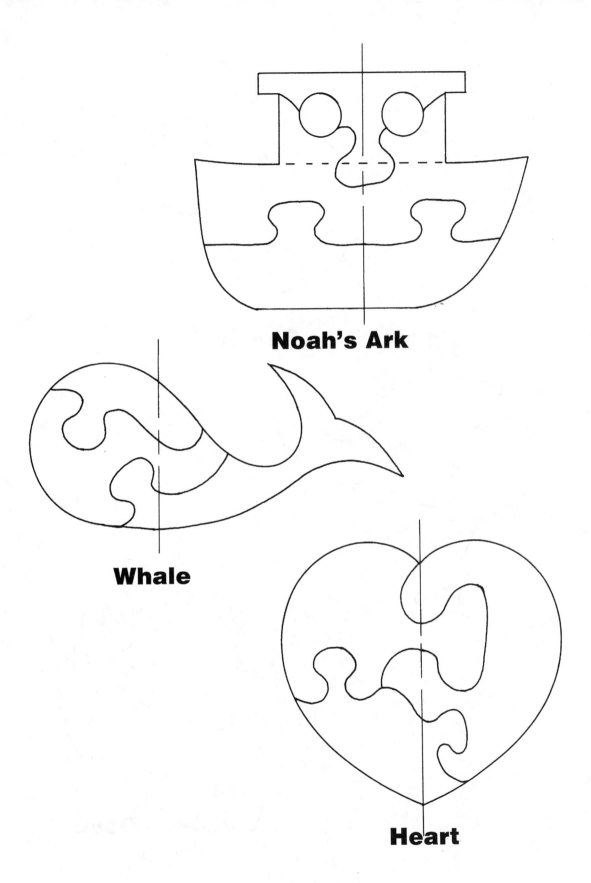

Noah's Ark

Whale

Heart

Seashell

Fish

Dove

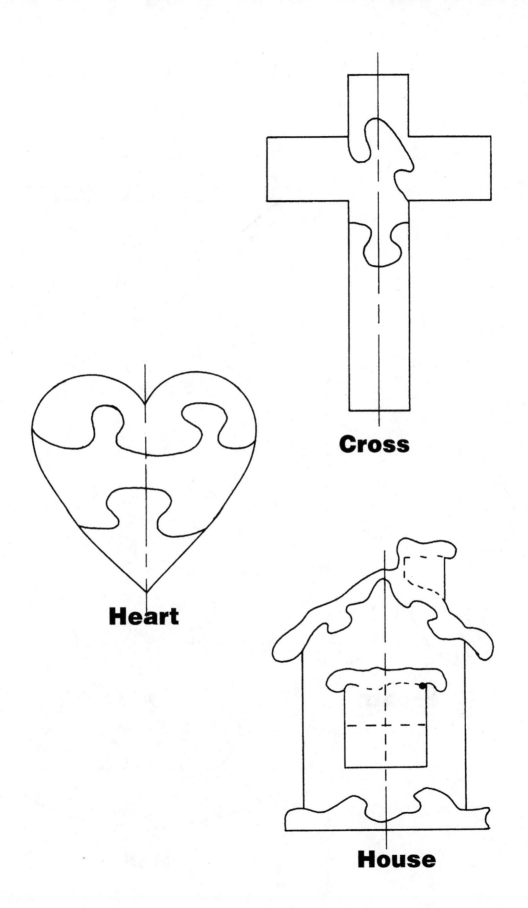

Cross

Heart

House

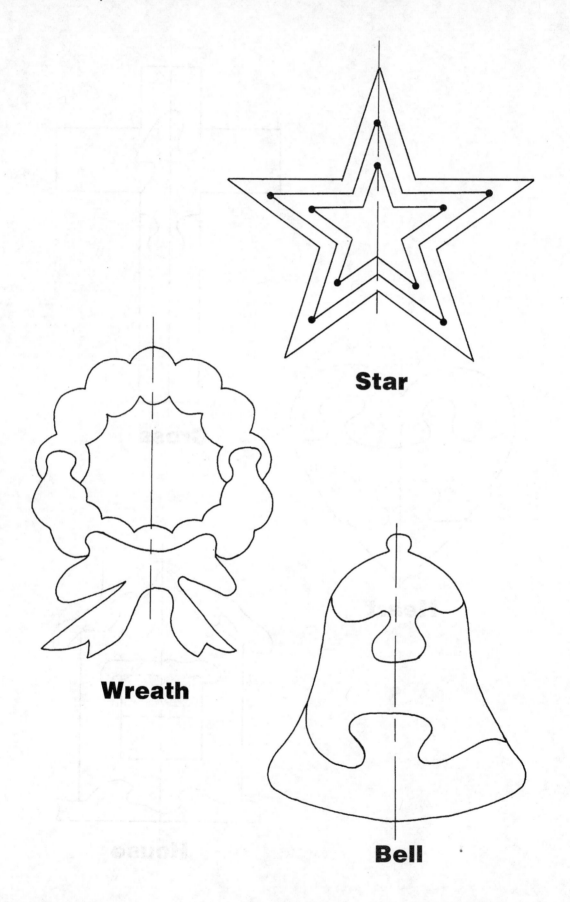

Star

Wreath

Bell

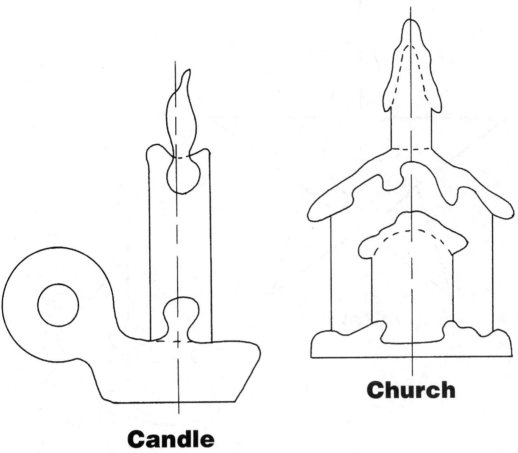

Candle

Church

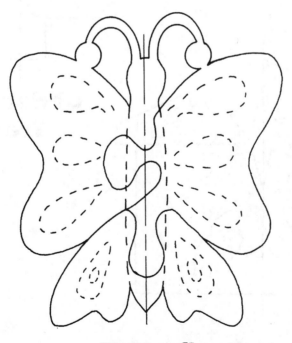

Butterfly

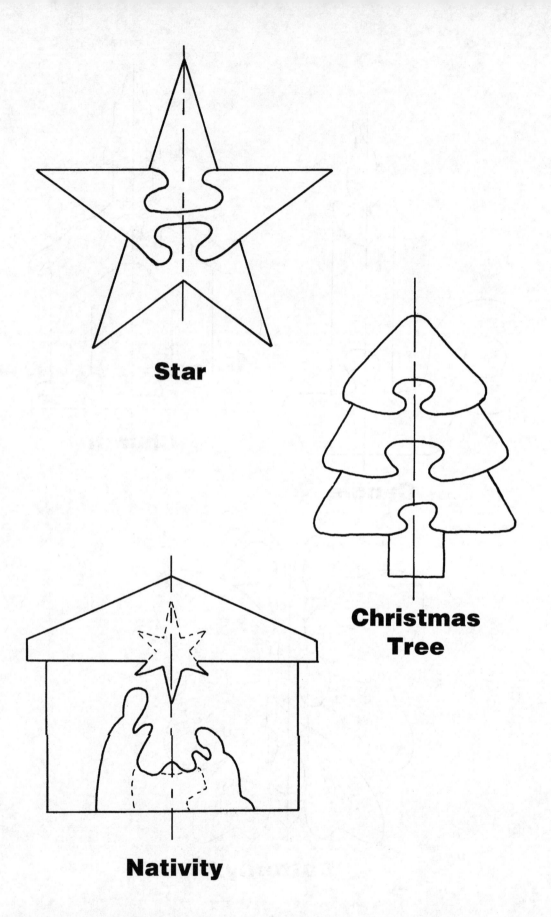

Star

Christmas Tree

Nativity

CHRISTMAS ORNAMENTS

Anchor Cross

Mission Cross

Bells

Shepherd's
Crook Cross

Nativity

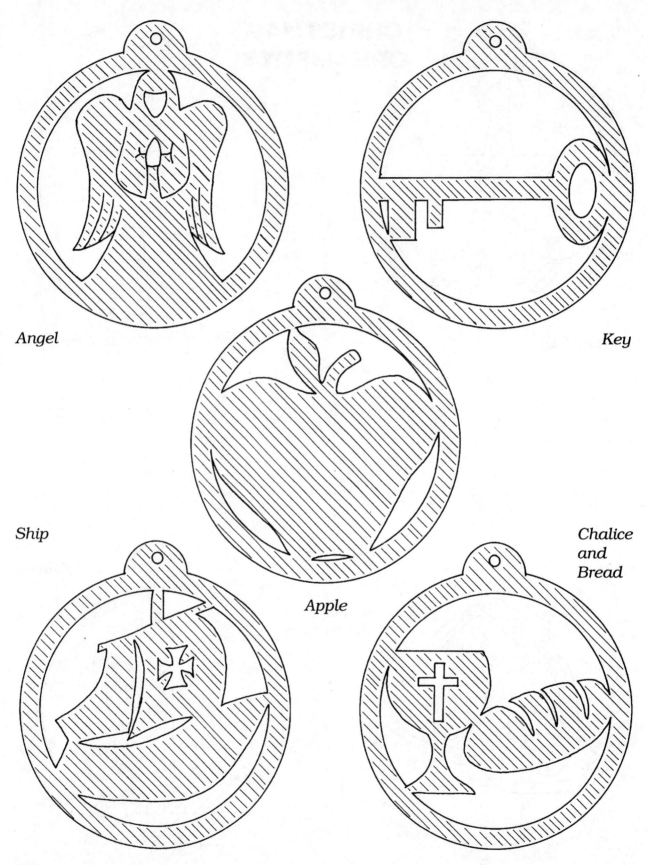

Angel

Key

Ship

Chalice
and
Bread

Apple

104

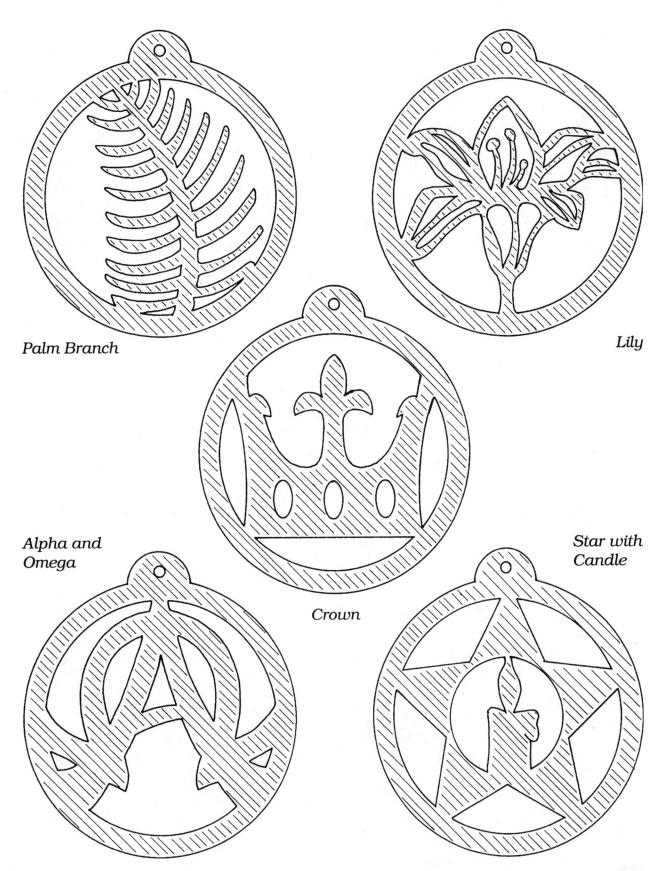

Palm Branch

Lily

Alpha and
Omega

Crown

Star with
Candle

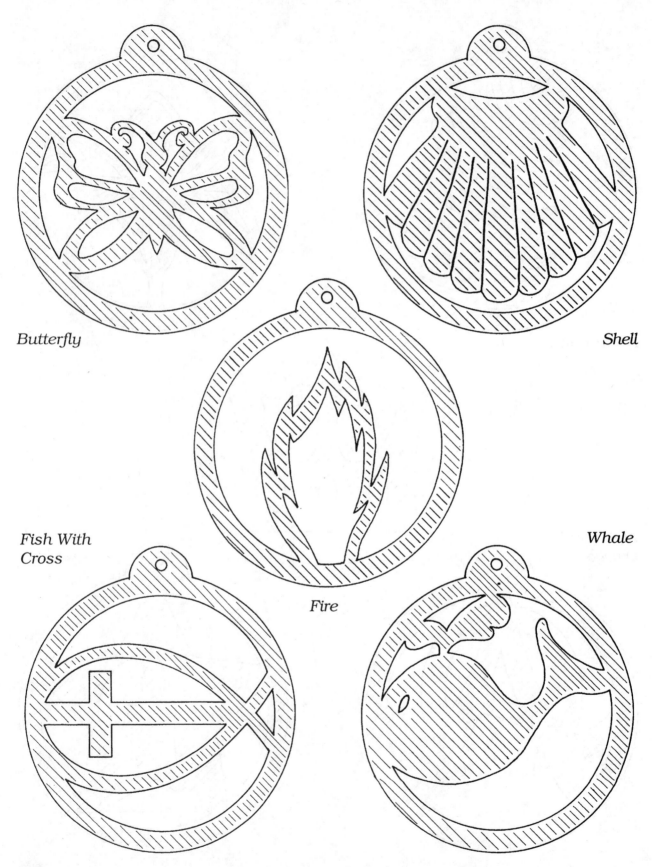

Butterfly

Shell

Fish With Cross

Fire

Whale

106

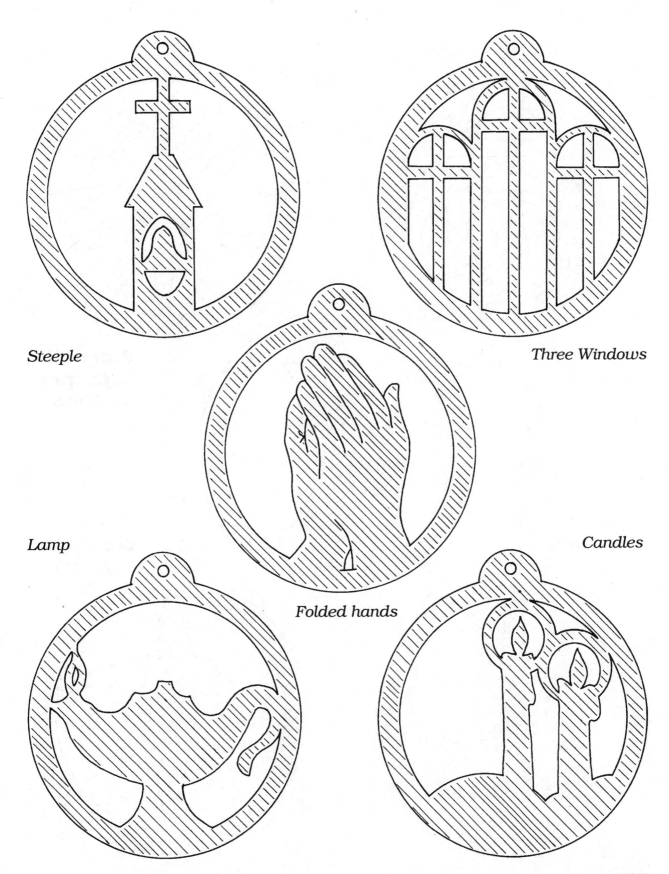

Steeple

Three Windows

Lamp

Candles

Folded hands

107

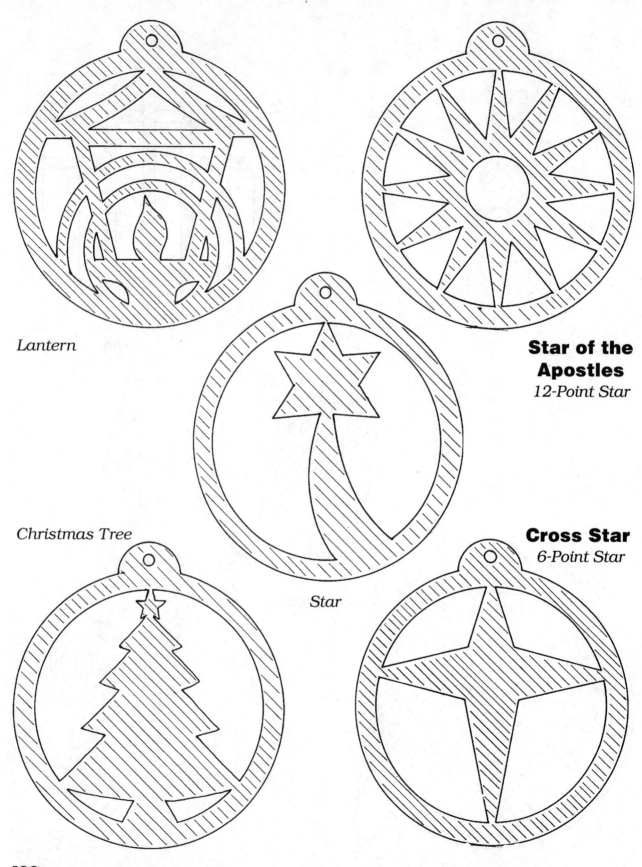

Lantern

Star of the
Apostles
12-Point Star

Christmas Tree

Star

Cross Star
6-Point Star

108

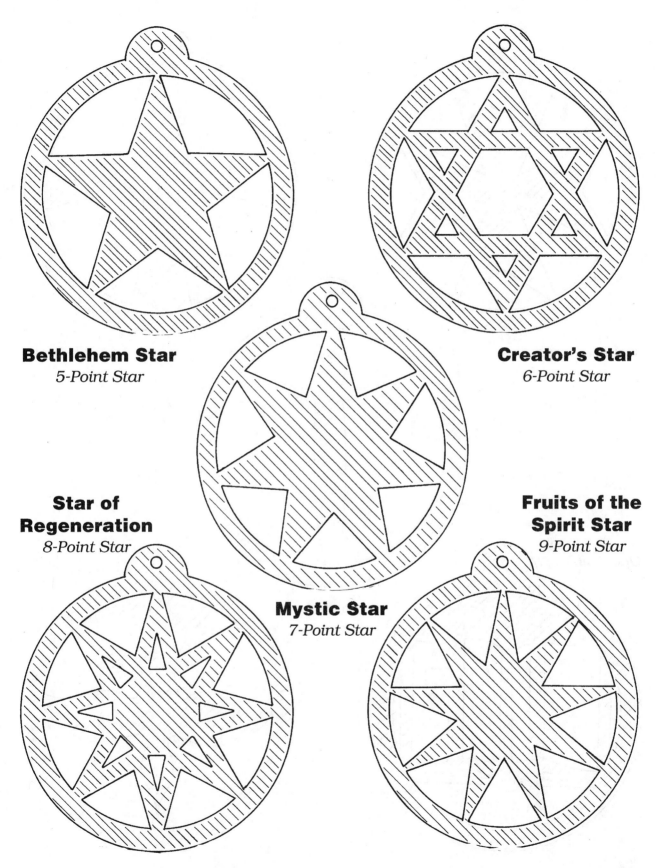

Bethlehem Star
5-Point Star

Creator's Star
6-Point Star

Star of Regeneration
8-Point Star

Fruits of the Spirit Star
9-Point Star

Mystic Star
7-Point Star

109

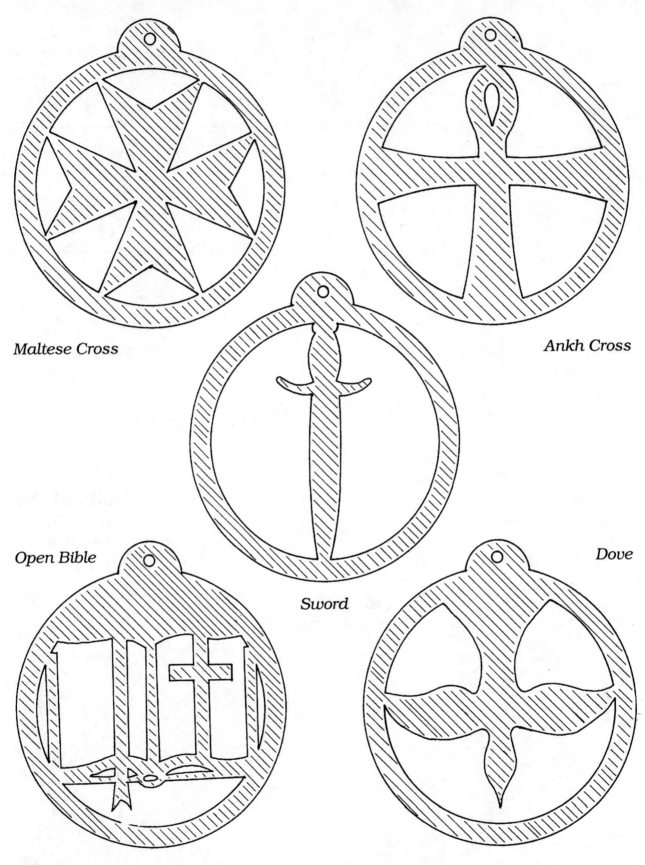

Maltese Cross

Ankh Cross

Open Bible

Sword

Dove

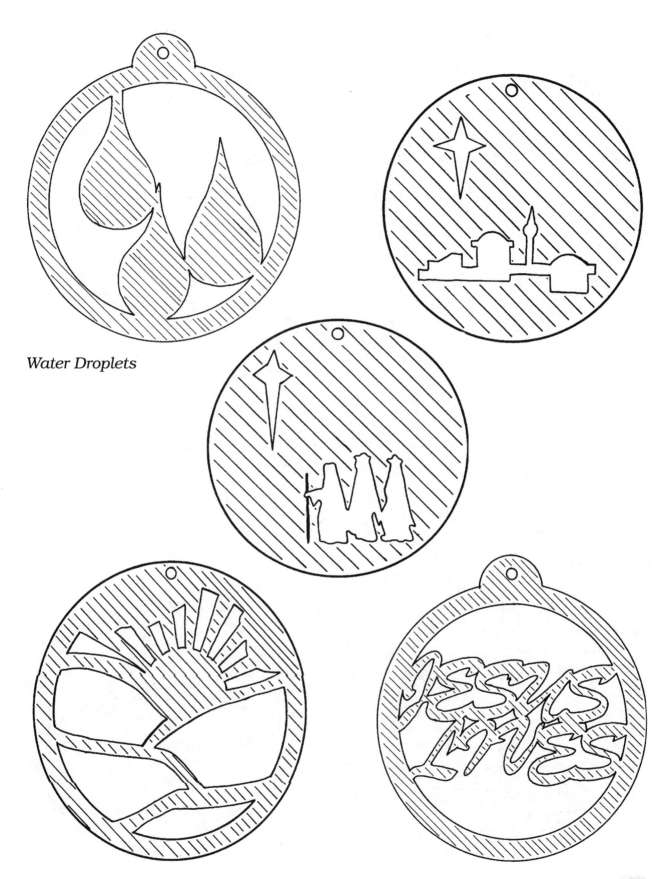

Water Droplets

111

112

113

114

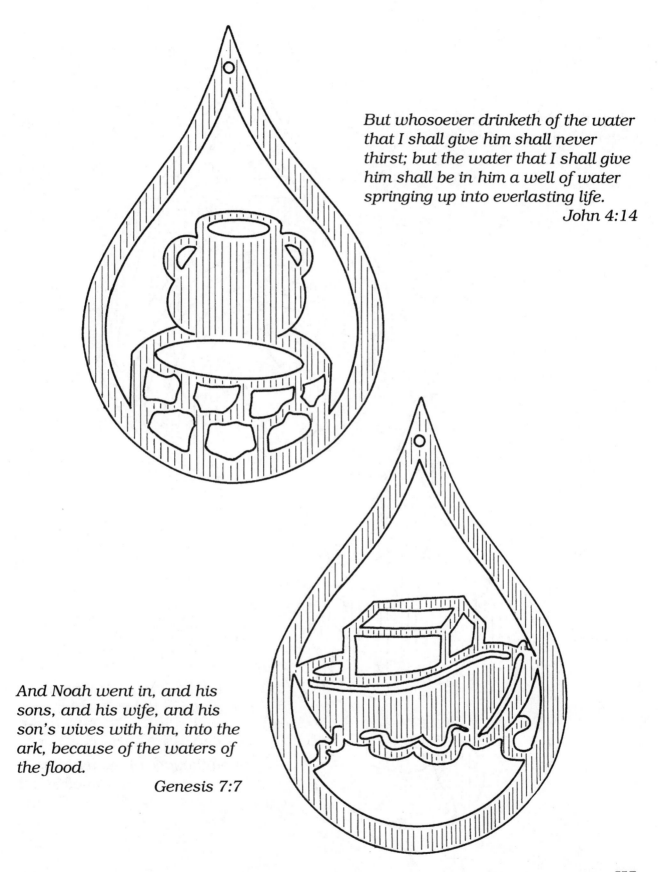

But whosoever drinketh of the water that I shall give him shall never thirst; but the water that I shall give him shall be in him a well of water springing up into everlasting life.

John 4:14

And Noah went in, and his sons, and his wife, and his son's wives with him, into the ark, because of the waters of the flood.

Genesis 7:7

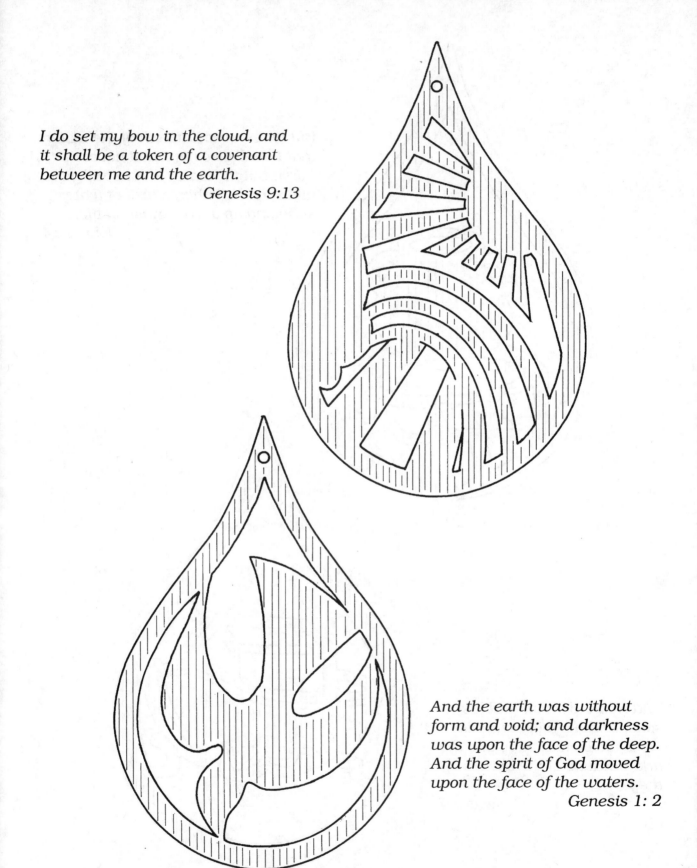

I do set my bow in the cloud, and it shall be a token of a covenant between me and the earth.

Genesis 9:13

And the earth was without form and void; and darkness was upon the face of the deep. And the spirit of God moved upon the face of the waters.

Genesis 1: 2

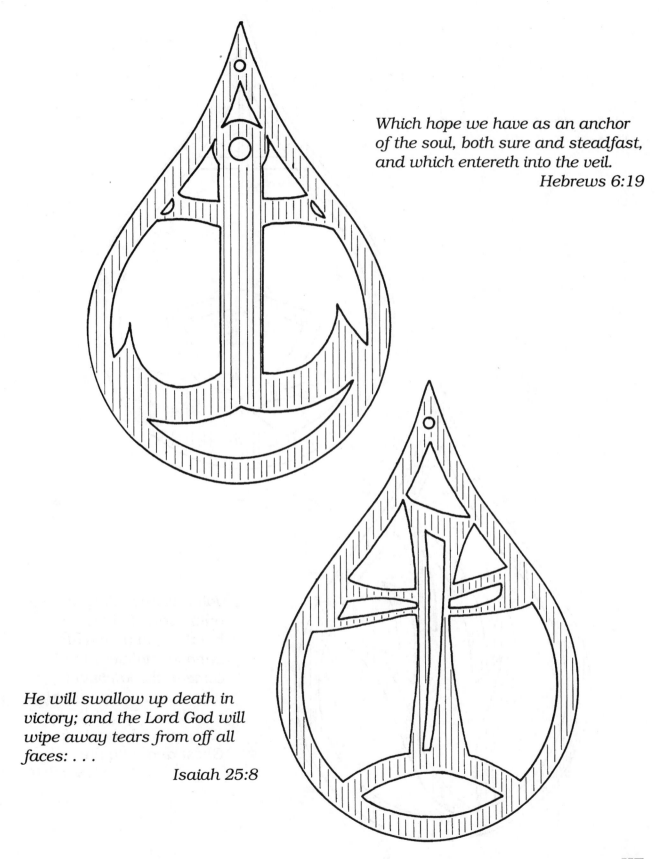

Which hope we have as an anchor of the soul, both sure and steadfast, and which entereth into the veil.

Hebrews 6:19

He will swallow up death in victory; and the Lord God will wipe away tears from off all faces: . . .

Isaiah 25:8

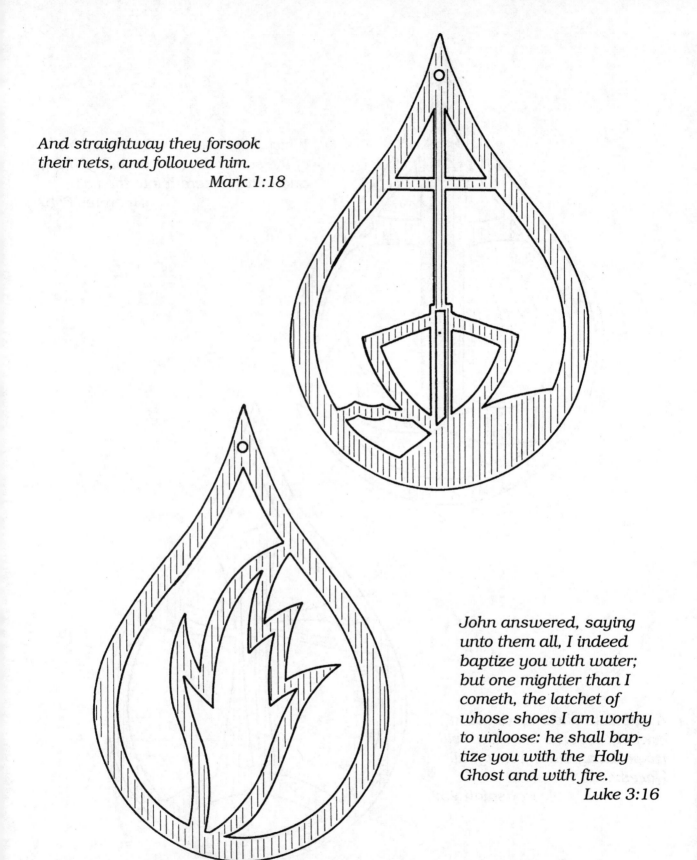

And straightway they forsook their nets, and followed him.

Mark 1:18

John answered, saying unto them all, I indeed baptize you with water; but one mightier than I cometh, the latchet of whose shoes I am worthy to unloose: he shall baptize you with the Holy Ghost and with fire.

Luke 3:16

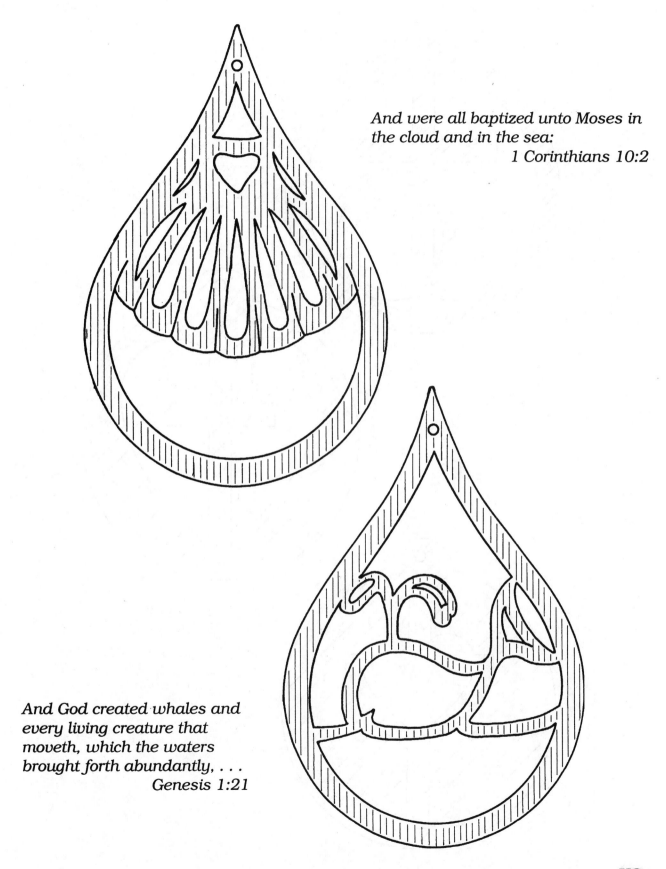

And were all baptized unto Moses in the cloud and in the sea:
1 Corinthians 10:2

And God created whales and every living creature that moveth, which the waters brought forth abundantly, . . .
Genesis 1:21

LETTER OPENERS

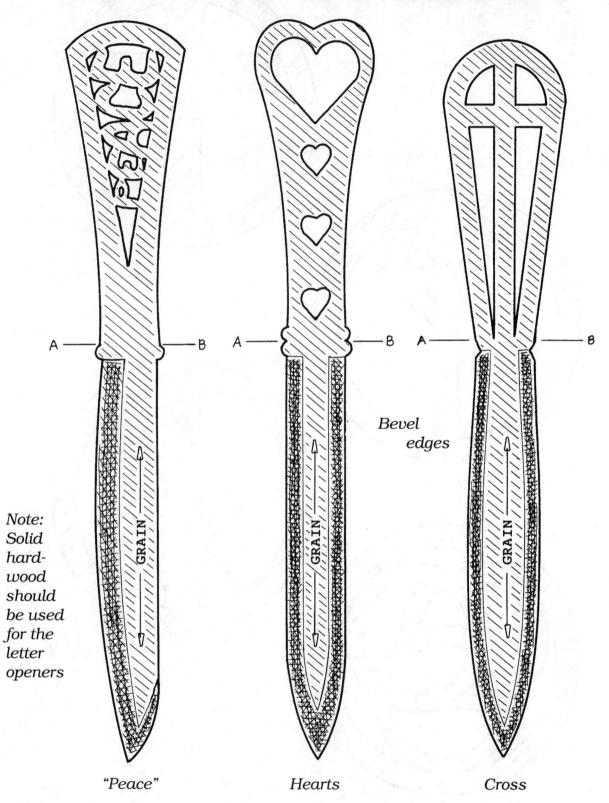

A ——— B

A ——— B

A ——— B

*Bevel
edges*

GRAIN

GRAIN

GRAIN

*Note:
Solid
hard-
wood
should
be used
for the
letter
openers*

"Peace"

Hearts

Cross

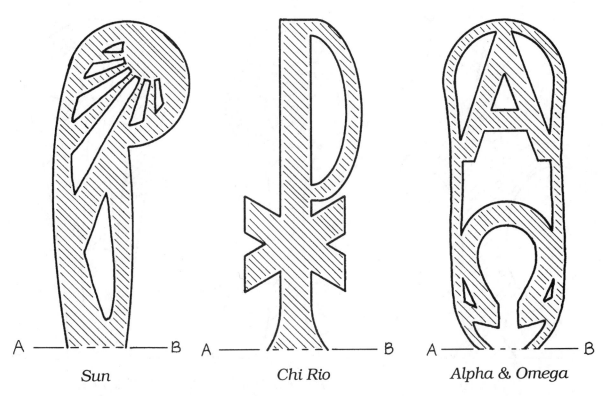

Sun

Chi Rio

Alpha & Omega

IXOYC: The Greek word for fish. It formed an acrostic of the Greek phrase "Jesus Christ", God's Son.

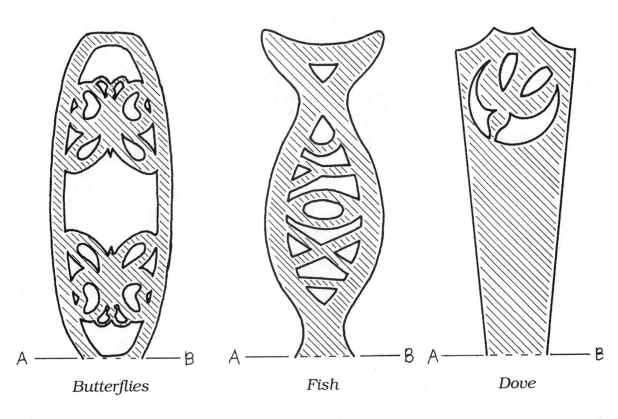

Butterflies

Fish

Dove

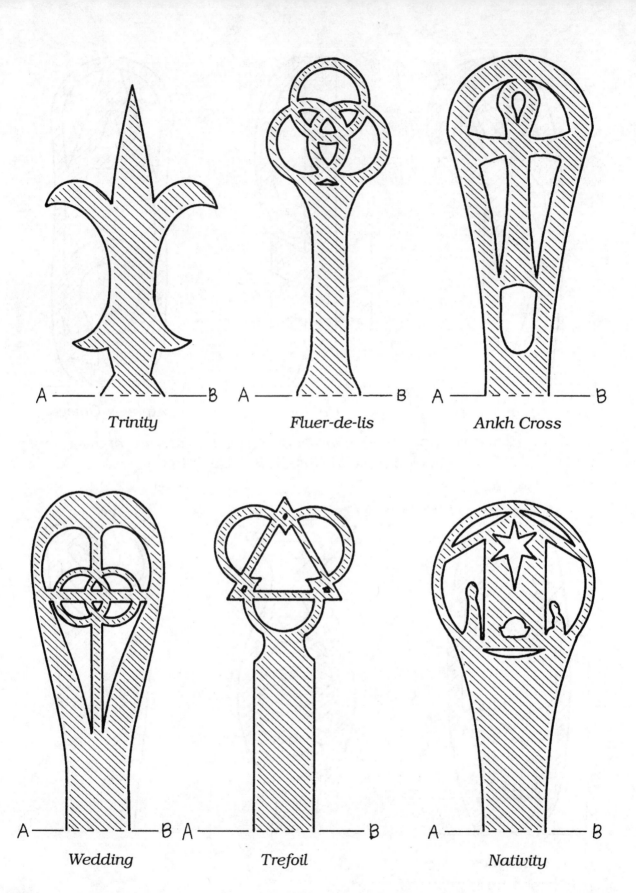

A ——————— B   A ——————— B   A ——————— B

Trinity   *Fluer-de-lis*   *Ankh Cross*

A ——————— B A ——————— B   A ——————— B

Wedding   *Trefoil*   *Nativity*

126

CHILDREN'S 3-DIMENSIONAL CUT-OUT PROJECTS

These projects require using 3/4" or 1" stock for best results. You'll find that these make sturdy, long-lasting playthings that children love!

Secure a small bell here in the steeple

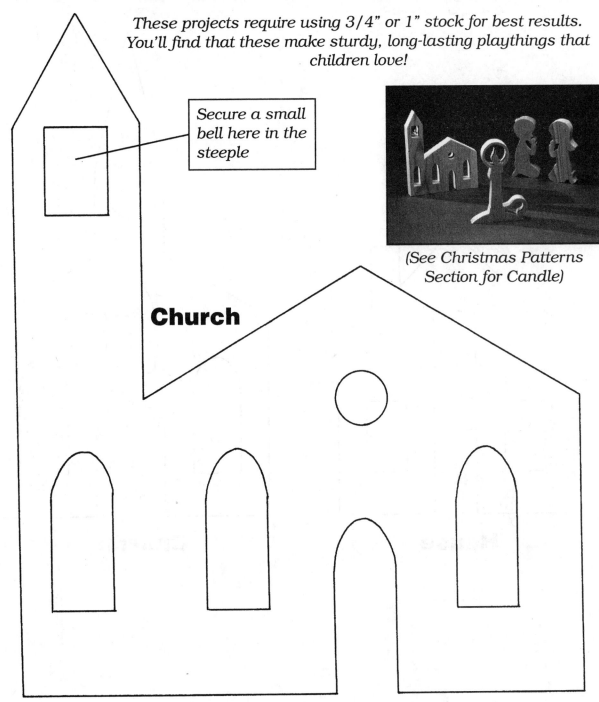

(See Christmas Patterns Section for Candle)

Church

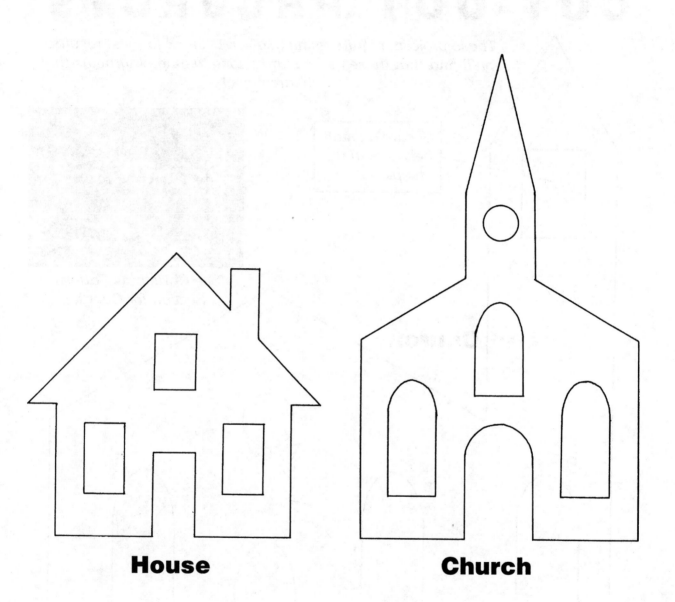

House   **Church**

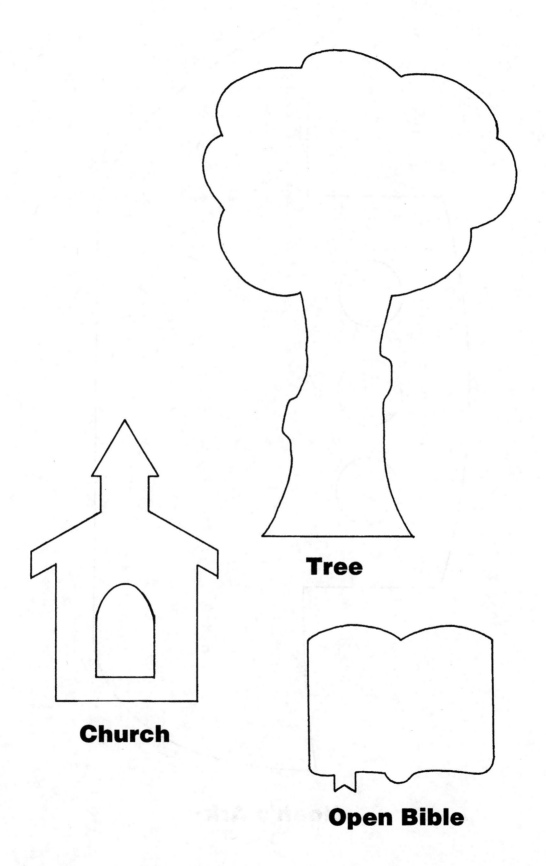

Tree

Church

Open Bible

129

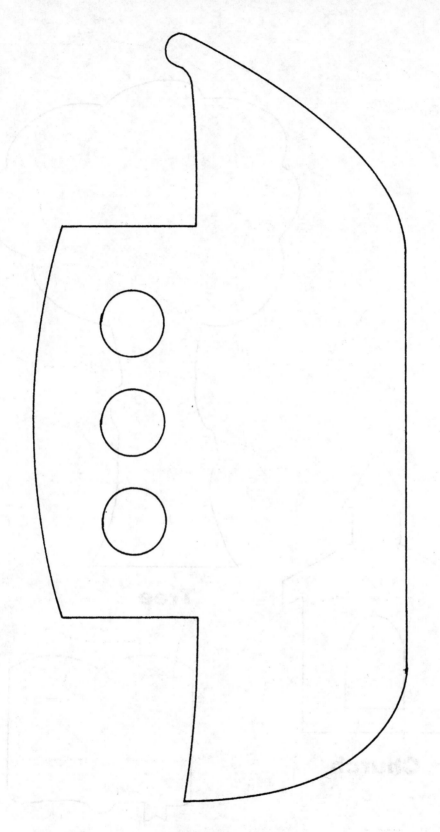

Noah's Ark

Dove

Hippopotamus

Sheep

Pig

Giraffe

Camel

Rainbow/ Clouds/ Sun

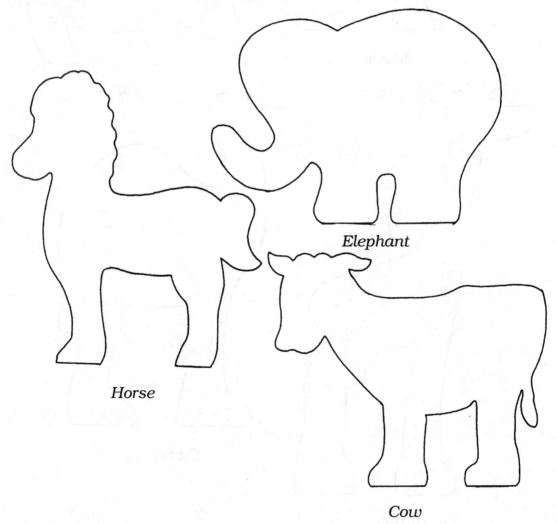

Elephant

Horse

Cow

These are popular projects for a child's room. Drill a hole in top for use as candle holders. They also make a nice set of bookends.

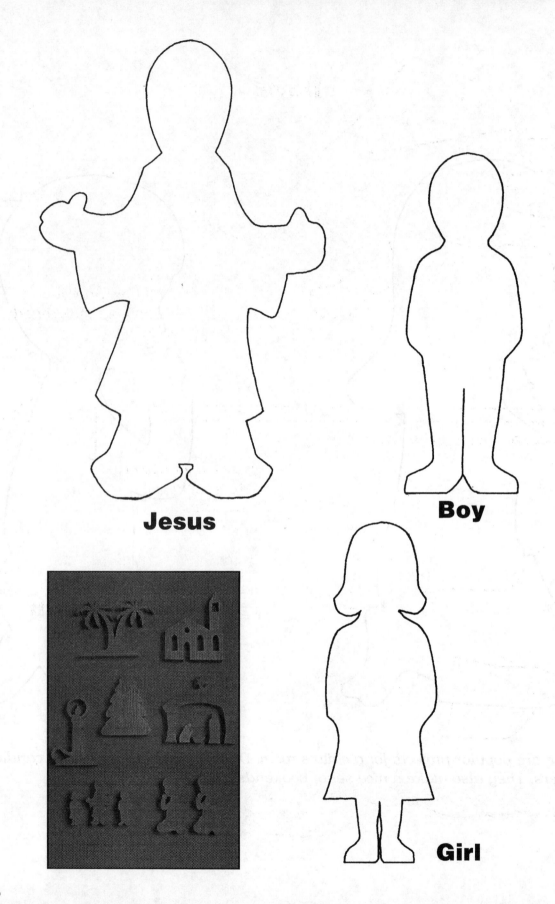

Jesus

Boy

Girl

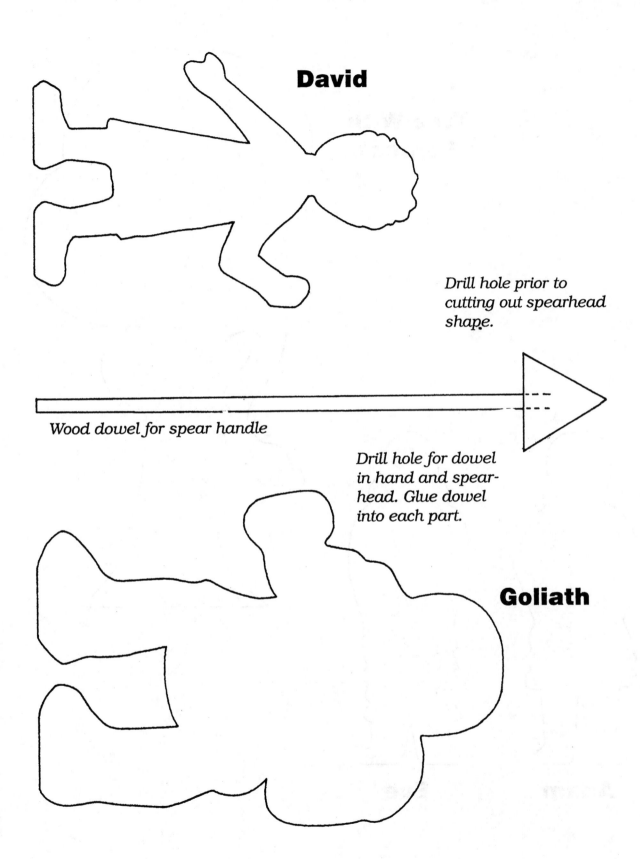

David

Drill hole prior to cutting out spearhead shape.

Wood dowel for spear handle

Drill hole for dowel in hand and spearhead. Glue dowel into each part.

Goliath

Tree With Serpent

Adam

Eve

Daniel and the Lions

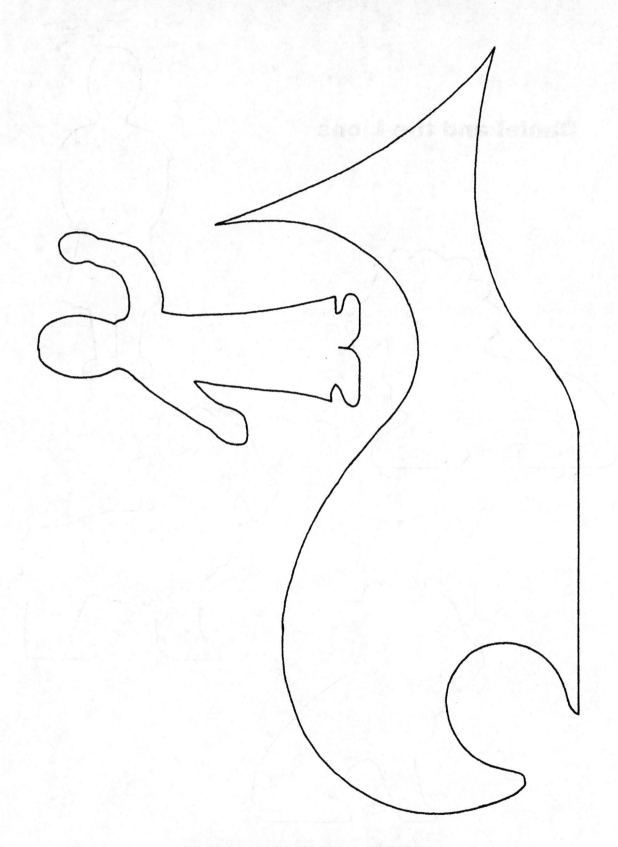

Jonah and the Whale

138

PUZZLES

1. Puzzles should be made from good-quality hardwood plywood 1/4" thick. Use two layers of wood: The top layer being of birch or maple plywood and the bottom layer of less expensive material.

Making these puzzles is an easy process. Cut the puzzle pieces out of the top layer. Glue the remaining border to the bottom layer to form a frame with backing for the puzzle pieces.

You can finish the puzzles in many different ways. You can choose no finish or you can use different oils, paints, or stain dyes. The best choice of finishing materials would be those that are non-toxic or that dry to form a non-toxic finish.

For additional information or to answer questions you may have about constructing puzzles, the following reference book should be consulted:

SCROLL SAW PUZZLE PATTERNS by Patrick and Patricia Spielman,
Sterling Publishing Company, 1988.

• *NOTE: Puzzle patterns should be enlarged by at least 165%.*

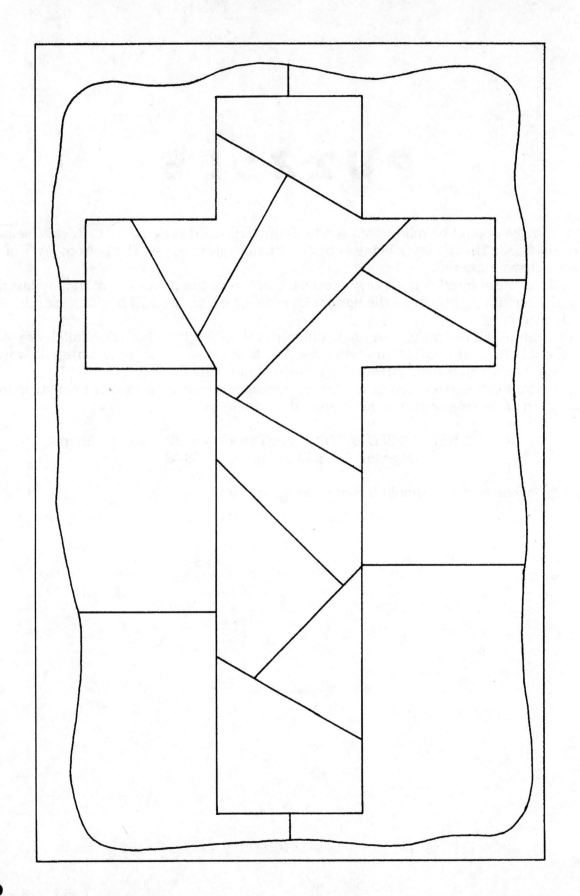

Noah's Ark — Genesis, Chapters 6-8

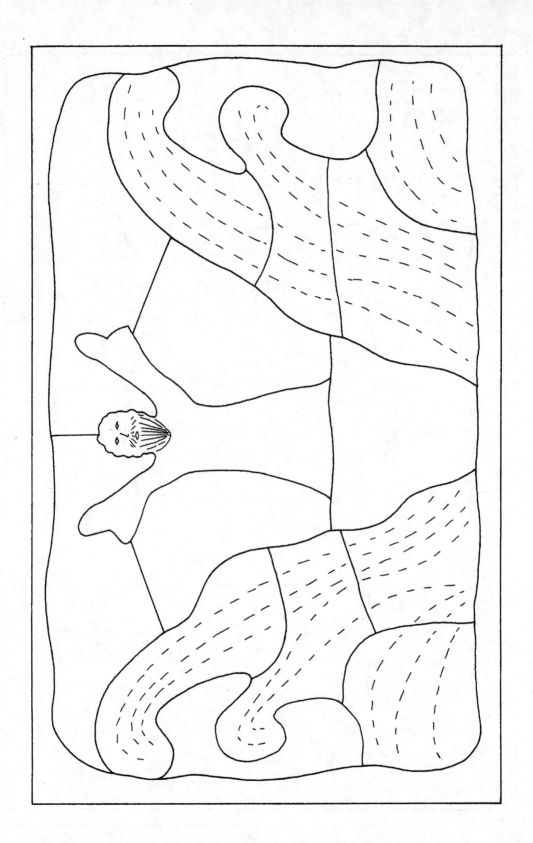

Moses Parting the Red Sea — Exodus, Chapter 14

Daniel in the Lion's Den— Daniel, Chapter 6

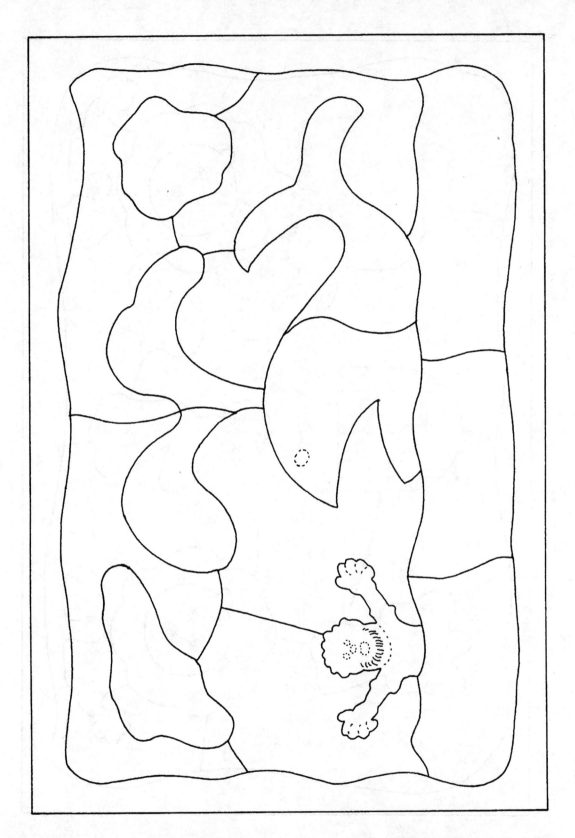

Jonah and the Whale— Jonah, Chapters 1-2

Jesus is Born — Luke, Chapter 2

Christ Has Risen— John, Chapters 18-20

LETTERS AND WORDS

The use of Greek letters to represent Jesus Christ is of very early origin. Because many of the first missionary churches were Greek, much of the New Testament was written in Greek.

The Greek alphabet contains 24 letters, so there is not a one-to-one correspondence with the English alphabet. For instance, since there is no letter "J" in the Greek alphabet, the letter "I" is used. The English equivalent of "E" is the Greek capital letter "H." Also the English letter "C" is a form of the Greek capital letter "S" (Sigma).

IHC or IHS

The first three letters of Jesus in Greek. Some Greek letters have several forms in English.

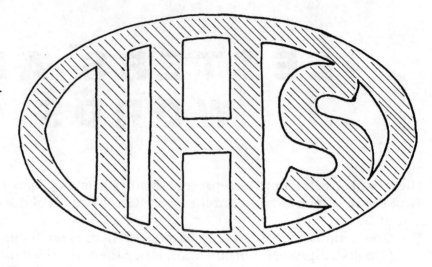

INRI

The first letters of the words in the Latin superscription, "Jesus Nazarenus Rex Iudaeorum" (Jesus of Nazareth, King of the Jews.) The superscription was on the upper part of the cross on which Jesus was crucified.

NIKA

The Greek word for conquer, conqueror or victor.

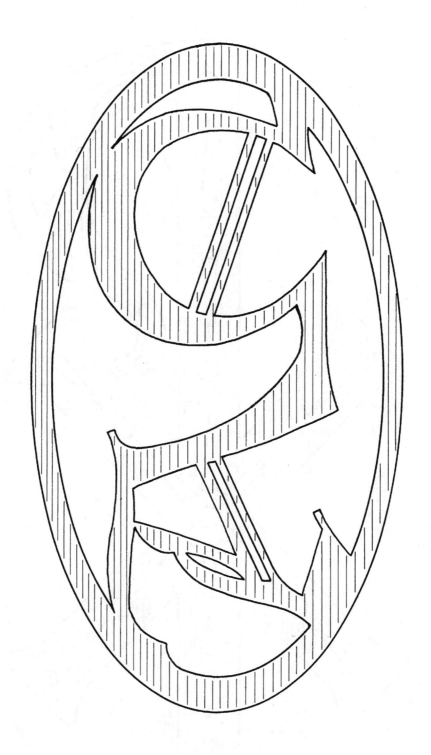

Alpha
Omega

Alpha and Omega have been added to emblems to symbolize the divinity of Christ since the fourth century. They are the first and last letters, representing the beginning and the end. (See Rev. 22:1)

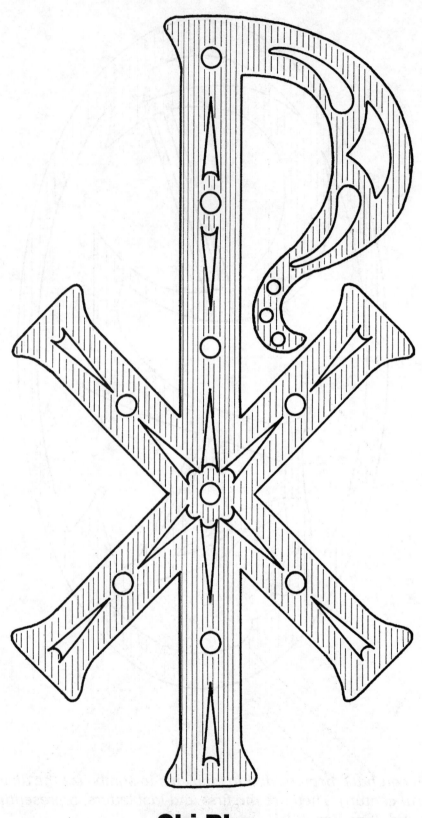

Chi Rho

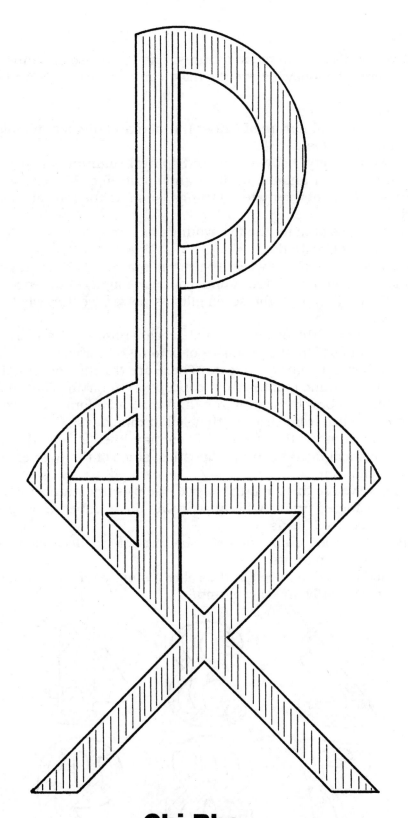

Chi Rho
Combined in a symbolic representation of Christ's birth.

Numbers

Numbers have significance in most cultures. The Bible also contains many examples of symbolic numbers. The following are the most common numbers and some of their symbolisms.

ONE: Unity; oneness; God

TWO: Refers to the dual nature of Christ (human and divine). It is also the division of unity; duality; and opposites.

THREE: The Holy Trinity; body, mind, and spirit; beginning, middle, and end; the threefold of nature (lower or animal, human, and spiritual or higher).

FOUR: Representative of the material things, such as the four elements (earth, air, fire, and water).

FIVE: The five senses of man; the five wounds of Christ.

SIX: The six days of Creation.

SEVEN: The seven days of the week; the seven heavens; the seven gifts of the Holy Spirit (Traditionally wisdom, understanding, counsel, might, knowledge, piety, and fear of the Lord). Revelation 5:12 lists the seven gifts as power, wealth, wisdom, might, honor, glory, and blessing.

EIGHT: The number of the octave - rebirth; regeneration at Baptism; the Resurrection; the eight Beatitudes (Christ's promises of coming blessings).

NINE: The number nine hardly appears. These are the nine orders of angels; Nine is a number of completion (nine months from conception to birth). The gates of Hell are thrice threefold; three of brass, three of iron, and three of adamantine rock. When the fallen angels were expelled from Heaven, they fell in nine days.

TEN: The perfect number; the number of commandments. Also the ten petals of the passion flower, a mystical meaning of the Apostles, since of the twelve, one denied the Lord and one betrayed him.

TWELVE: The twelve prophets and the twelve disciples; the number of months in a year.

THIRTEEN: Considered unlucky because it was the number of people at the Last Supper, where one betrayed Jesus.

FIFTEEN: Progress; the number of steps the Virgin Mary ascended when she entered the Temple on leaving her parents.

FORTY: A period of trial; as used in the Bible it simply refers to a "long time" or a "great many," not necessarily an exact number.

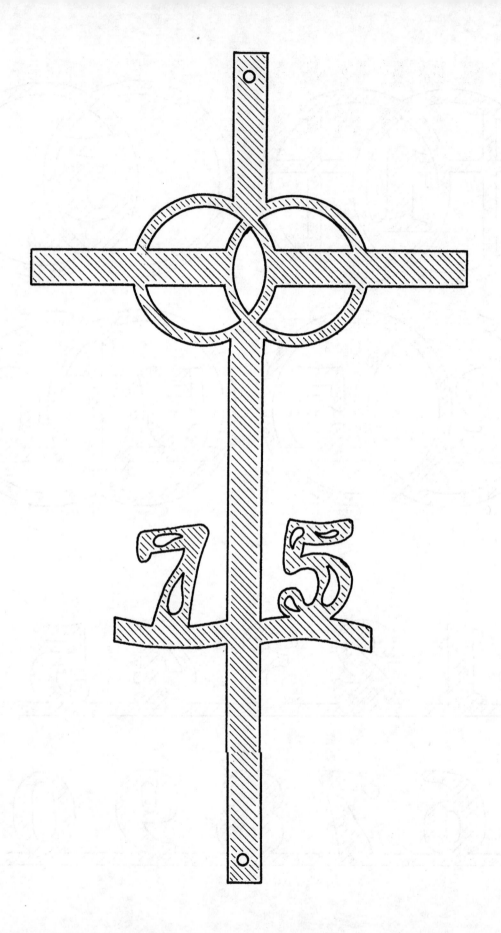

154

GENERAL PATTERN TREASURY

156

The Lamb of God

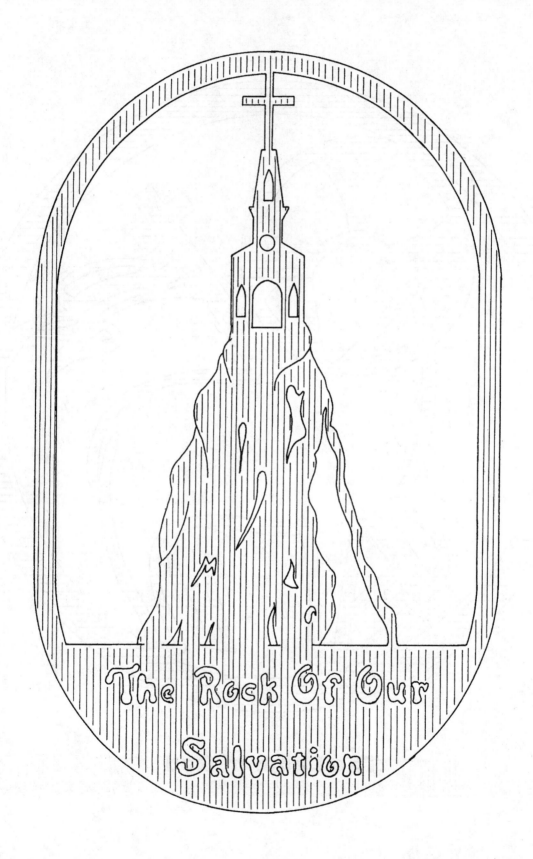

The Rock Of Our Salvation

159

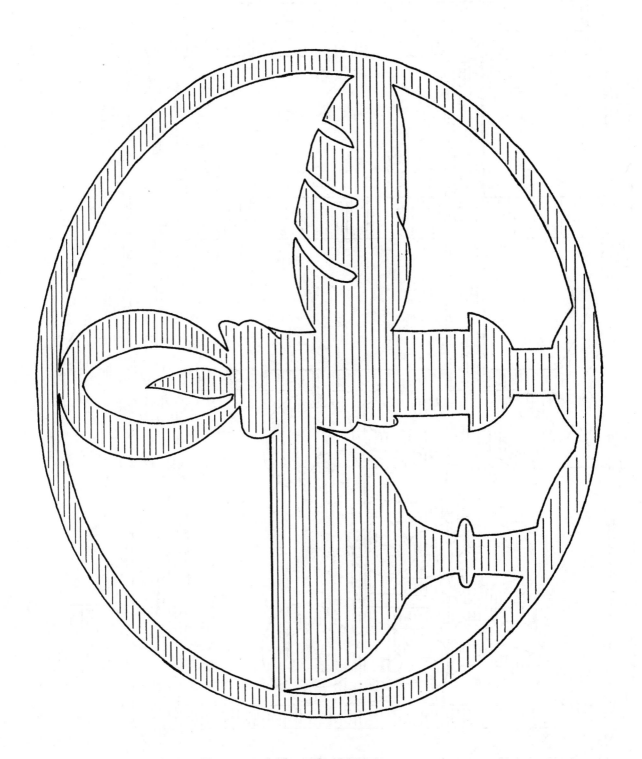

161

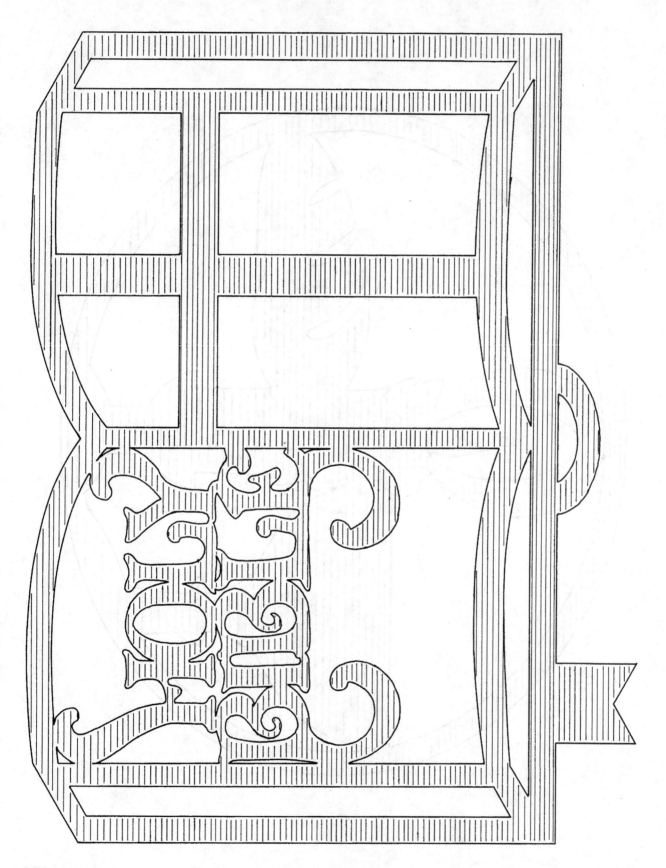

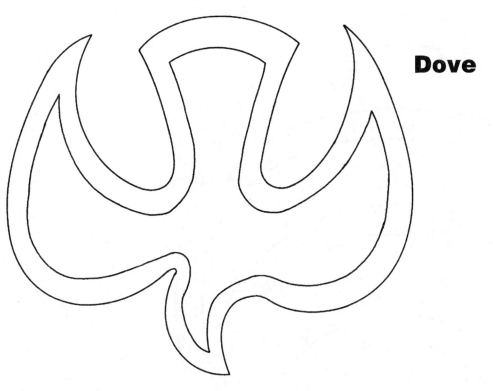

Dove

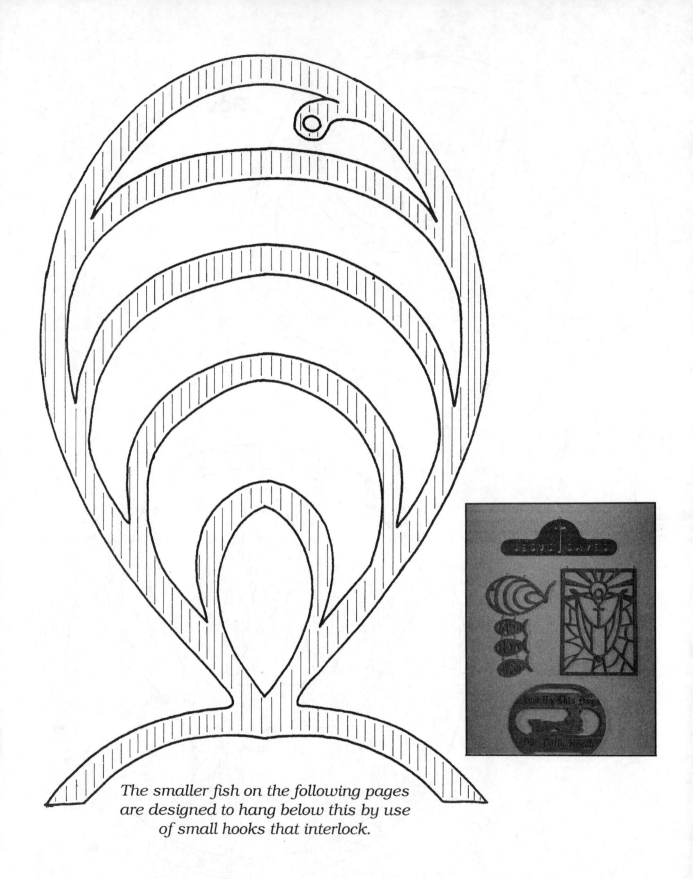

The smaller fish on the following pages
are designed to hang below this by use
of small hooks that interlock.

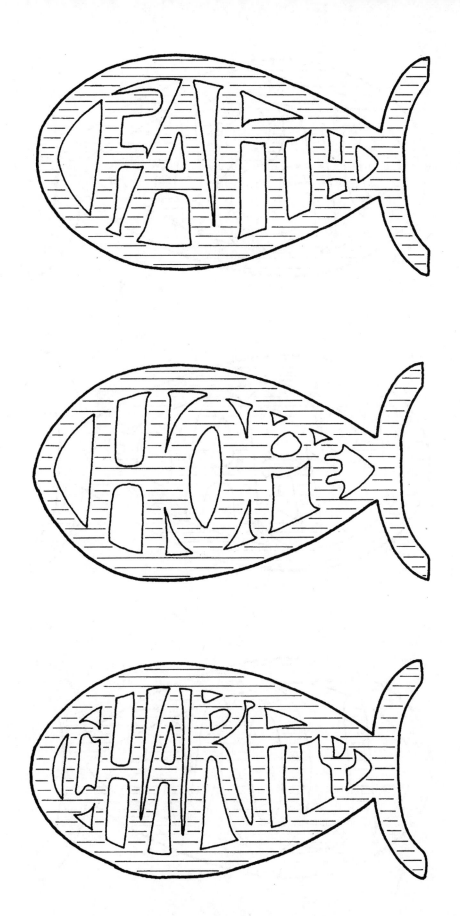

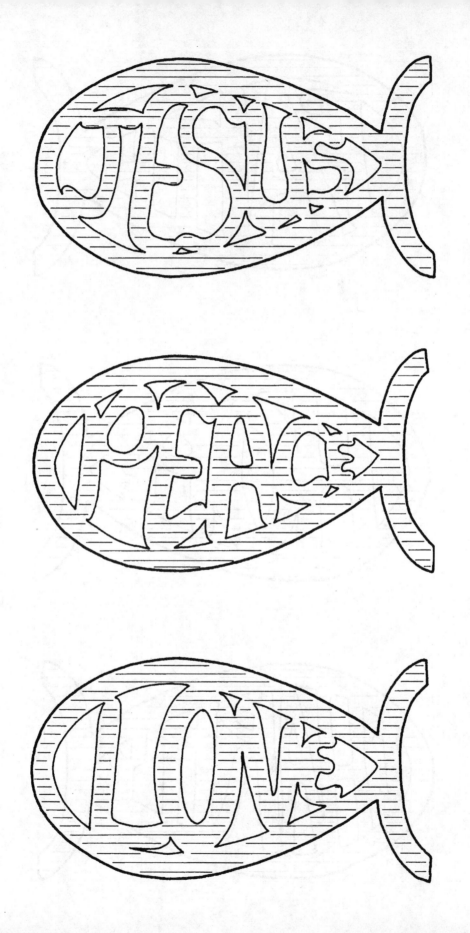

167

Last Supper (Left Hand)

Last Supper (Right Hand)

BIBLIOGRAPHY

Advanced Bible History (13th printing) (1936). St. Louis: Concordia Publishing House.

Baldock, John. (1990). *The Elements of Christian Symbolism*. Great Britain: Element Books Limited.

Blake, Willson W. (1888). *The Cross, Ancient and Modern*. New York: Anson D.F. Randolf and Co.

Cross, F.L., and E.A. Livinstone. (1974). *The Oxford Dictionary of the Christian Church*. New York: Oxford University Press.

Holy Bible. Concordia Publishing House.

Hulme, F. Edward. (1899). *Symbolism in Christian Art*. New York: MacMillian Co.

Koch, Rudolf. (1955). *The Book of Signs*. New York: Dover Publications, Inc.

Krythe, Maymie Richardson. (1954). *All About Christmas*. New York: Harper and Brothers.

Laliberte, Norman, and Edward N. West. (1960). *The History of the Cross*. New York: The MacMillan Co.

Lauckner, Edie. (1978). *Signs of Celebration*. St. Louis: Concordia Publishing House.

Moe, Dean. (1985). *Christian Symbols Handbook*. Minneapolis: Augsburg Publishing House.

Rest, Freidrich O. (1954). *Our Christian Symbols*. Cleveland: The Pilgrim Press.

Sears, Fern. (1953). *Let Me Speak—The Language of Christian Symbols*. Kansas City: Brown-White-Lowell Press.

Smith's Bible Dictionary. Philadelphia: A.J. Holman Co.

Stafford, Thomas Albert. (1942). *Christian Symbolism in the Evangelical Churches*. New York: Abingdon-Cokesbury Press.

Webber, F.R. (1971). *Church Symbolism* (2nd Ed.). Detroit: Gale Research Company.

Wetzler, Robert P., and Helen Huntington. (1962). *Seasons and Symbols*. Minneapolis: Augsburg Publishing House.

APPENDIX A
BOOKS ON SCROLL SAW BASICS AND ITS USE

SCROLL SAW HANDBOOK by Patrick Spielman, Sterling Publishing Co.; 1986.

PATTERNS AND PROJECTS FOR THE SCROLL SAW by Joyce C. Nelson and John A. Nelson, Stackpole Books, 1991.

SCROLL SAW FRETWORK TECHNIQUES AND PROJECTS by Patrick Spielman and James Reidle, Sterling Publishing Co. 1990.

CHRISTMAS SCROLL SAW PATTERNS by Patrick and Patricia Spielman, Sterling Publishing Co. 1992.

SCROLL SAW FRETWORK PATTERNS by Patrick Spielman and James Reidle, Sterling Publishing Co. 1989.

Books from the Experts
Fox Chapel Publishing

Carving the Full Moon Saloon with the Caricature Carvers of America. Patterns ideas and techniques from some of the best carvers alive- Harold Enlow, Tom Wolfe, Desiree Hajny, Steve Prescott, Pete LeClair, Bob Travis and 15 more. Over 100 color photos show close up details, painting tips and more. THE book for caricature carvers. $19.95

Carving Clowns with Jim Maxwell. Capture the humor and mystery! 12 different clowns through the ages. Color painting section and project gallery. $12.95

Bark Carving by Joyce Buchanan. Full color step-by-step guide includes finishing details and 12 + patterns. $12.95

Carving Fish- Miniature Salt water and Freshwater by Jim Jensen. These detailed patterns, woodburning tips, color painting section and step-by-step photos show you how to carve 26 different miniature fish for sale or display. $14.95

Sculpturing Totem Poles by Walt Way. This classic guide to understanding and carving totem poles is now back in print. Highly recommended. $6.95

Small INTARSIA Projects- by Judy Gale Roberts. Full color technique and pattern manual featuring 12 + new patterns for jewelry, small boxes and more! $14.95

Christian Designs for the Scroll Saw
Inside are 300 + patterns for jewelry, ornaments, plaques, crosses and more. These precise drawings could be used for relief carving and pierced carvings as well. 30 projects in color. $14.95

Mott Miniature Furniture Workshop Manual. Ready to use patterns for 144 projects, 220 pages. $19.95

Animal Books by Chip Chats columnist Mary Duke Guldan
Woodcarvers Workbook- Carving animals with Mary Duke Guldan. Step-by-Step instructions and the best patterns you've ever seen! 9 patterns-including Wolves, Whitetails, Wild Horses, Moose, Rabbit, Dogs. $14.95

Woodcarver's Workbooks #2 More Great Projects No repeats from book #1 above, patterns including Buffalo, Bears, Elk, Native Chief, Horses, Mules, Oxen . . . and more $14.95

Mammals: An Artistic Approach by Desiree Hajny. step by step photographs and color painting section teach you Desiree's secrets to her world class carving. Patterns included for otter, bear, deer. . . $19.95

Fantastic Book of Canes, Pipes and Walking Sticks by Harry Ameredes. 100's of detailed designs. Including weathered wood tree-root designs and pipes. $12.95

Making Collectible Santas and Christmas Ornaments. 42 easy to follow projects. Hand carved- ornaments are popular! $6.95

Carving Characters with Jim Maxwell. Twelve favorite projects from the Ozark Mountains $6.95

Carving Wooden Critters by Diane Ernst. 16 projects and step-by-step section. Rabbits, puppies, otters, & more in her unique caricature style. Great designs! $6.95

Carving Kids- Ivan Whillock. Step-by-step techniques and patterns for 12 carved children. $12.95

Woodcarving Adventure Movie Caricatures with Jim Maxwell. His best book yet! 150 + step-by-step photos. 20 + patterns. $12.95

Easy to Make Inlay Wood Projects- INTARSIA THE book on this type of relief woodworking for scroll and band saw users. 15 free patterns included, 30 projects in color. $19.95

Scroll Saw Woodcrafting Magic by Joanne Lockwood. 300 page project and instruction book. 30 pages of lettering and alphabets. Color painting instructions $16.95

Bird Carving Encyclopedia of Bird Reference Drawings- by Mohrhardt. Detailed sketches and info on 215 different birds. Recommended by Barth, Guge. $14.95

George Lehman Carving books Detailed life-size patterns. For books- buy individually or save on set! 4 Book George Lehman set (see titles below). $69.95

Book #1- Carving 20 Realistic Game and Songbirds. Includes loon, chickadee, owl, mallard . . . $19.95

Book #2- Realism in Wood- 22 patterns Special buying info, includes bald eagle, pheasants, teals . . . $19.95

Book #3- Nature in Wood 21 small birds and 8 animal patterns. Songbird and other small birds. Many tips and techniques. $16.95

Book #4- Carving Wildlife in Wood Includes shorebirds, wild turkey, geese, heron, osprey $19.95

How to Order: Please send price plus $2.00 per book postage (maximum $5.00 shipping)

Fox Chapel Publishing
Box 7948 G
Lancaster, PA 17604-7948
FAX (717) 560-4702
Toll free Order Desk- 1(800)457-9112